Access to History

General Editor: Keith Randell

The British Empire 1815-1914

Frank McDonough

Hodder & Stoughton

A MEMBER OF THE HODDER HEADLINE GROUP

The cover illustration is a map of the British Empire in 1886.
(Courtesy of The Mansell Collection.)

Some other titles in the series:

Tories, Conservatives and Unionists 1815-1914   ISBN 0 340 60081 0
Duncan Watts

Labour and Reform: Working Class Movements 1815-1914   ISBN 0 340 52930 X
Clive Behagg

Rivalry and Accord: International Relations 1870-1914   ISBN 0 340 51806 5
John Lowe

Britain: Domestic Politics 1939-64   ISBN 0 340 59256 7
Paul Adelman

Britain: Foreign and Imperial Affairs 1939-64   ISBN 0 340 59702 X
Alan Farmer

To Ann and Emily, with love and thanks
and to the memory of my mother - Alice

British Library Cataloguing in Publication Data

McDonough, Frank
    British Empire, 1815-1914. - (Access to
    History Series)
    I. Title II. Series
    909.0917241

ISBN 0-340-59376-8

First published 1994

Impression number   10 9 8 7 6
Year   2003

Typeset by Sempringham publishing, Bedford
Printed in Great Britain for Hodder & Stoughton Educational, a division of Hodder
Headline, 338 Euston Road, London NW1 3BH
by CPI Bath.

Contents

Preface

To the general reader

Although the *Access to History* series has been designed with the needs of students studying the subject at higher examination levels very much in mind, it also has a great deal to offer the general reader. The main body of the text (i.e. ignoring the Study Guides at the ends of chapters) forms a readable and yet stimulating survey of a coherent topic as studied by historians. However, each author's aim has not merely been to provide a clear explanation of what happened in the past (to interest and inform): it has also been assumed that most readers wish to be stimulated into thinking further about the topic and to form opinions of their own about the significance of the events that are described and discussed (to be challenged). Thus, although no prior knowledge of the topic is expected on the reader's part, she or he is treated as an intelligent and thinking person throughout. The author tends to share ideas and possibilities with the reader, rather than passing on numbers of so-called 'historical truths'.

To the student reader

There are many ways in which the series can be used by students studying History at a higher level. It will, therefore, be worthwhile thinking about your own study strategy before you start your work on this book. Obviously, your strategy will vary depending on the aim you have in mind, and the time for study that is available to you.

If, for example, you want to acquire a general overview of the topic in the shortest possible time, the following approach will probably be the most effective:

1 Read chapter 1 and think about its contents.
2 Read the 'Making notes' section at the end of chapter 2 and decide whether it is necessary for you to read this chapter.
3 If it is, read the chapter, stopping at each heading to note down the main points that have been made.
4 Repeat stage 2 (and stage 3 where appropriate) for all the other chapters.

If, however, your aim is to gain a thorough grasp of the topic, taking however much time is necessary to do so, you may benefit from carrying out the same procedure with each chapter, as follows:

1 Read the chapter as fast as you can, and preferably at one sitting.
2 Study the flow diagram at the end of the chapter, ensuring that you understand the general 'shape' of what you have just read.

3 Read the 'Making notes' section (and the 'Answering essay questions' section, if there is one) and decide what further work you need to do on the chapter. In particularly important sections of the book, this will involve reading the chapter a second time and stopping at each heading to think about (and to write a summary of) what you have just read.

4 Attempt the 'Source-based questions' section. It will sometimes be sufficient to think through your answers, but additional understanding will often be gained by forcing yourself to write them down.

When you have finished the main chapters of the book, study the 'Further Reading' section and decide what additional reading (if any) you will do on the topic.

This book has been designed to help make your studies both enjoyable and successful. If you can think of ways in which this could have been done more effectively, please write to tell me. In the meantime, I hope that you will gain greatly from your study of History.

Keith Randell

Acknowledgements

The Publishers would like to thank the following for permission to reproduce illustrations in this volume:

Cover - by courtesy of the Mansell Collection, London.

Wilberforce House, Hull City Museums and Art Galleries p 16; Mansell Collection, London p 31; Punch Publications p 100.

Every effort has been made to trace and acknowledge ownership of copyright. The Publishers will be glad to make suitable arrangements with any copyright holders whom it has not been possible to contact.

CHAPTER 1

Introduction: The British Empire, 1815-1914

At its height the British Empire was territorially the largest empire in world history. In 1914 its population of over 400 million people was to be found in all regions of the globe, in places as diverse as India, Egypt, Malaya, the West Indies, Australia and Canada (see the map on page 113). Yet within 60 years it had disintegrated into a plethora of independent states. The study of the British Empire - viewed 100 years ago as an essential part of the education of every school child in Britain - has for more than a generation now been looked upon with a mixture of embarrassment and indifference by the overwhelming majority of the British people.

Yet among historians the study of British imperialism has enjoyed a remarkable renaissance in recent years. New scholarly studies have appeared in rapid succession on matters such as the costs and benefits of the Empire, business and Empire, and the impact of the Empire on British politics, society and popular culture. Large numbers of Indian, West Indian, Asian, African, Canadian, and Australian historians are bringing fresh insights, new theories and enlivening new approaches to the study of British imperialism. It seems that wherever you look within historical study at present the Empire is, for good or ill, striking back.

But there have been few short and accessible studies which have kept pace with all this new research. This book aims to fill the gap by providing a brief introduction to the development of the British Empire between 1815 and 1914. In a book of this size it would, of course, be impossible to deal with every event in every colony. The study of a topic as large as the British Empire must of necessity be highly selective. The history of the Empire is really the story of numerous divergent developments. Nevertheless, it is hoped that all the major events, regions and themes, and all the most important recent historiographical debates have been found a place in this volume.

1 Empires and Imperialism: Some Definitions

a) Empires

Definition is extremely important in the study of any empire. This is because an empire is something very different from a nation. A nation is usually comprised of people with a common language, religion, and political institutions; a clear geographical location; and exact borders. As the British Empire consisted of people with very different languages, religions, and political institutions scattered around the world, the Empire cannot be studied as if it were a nation.

A separate definition is therefore required to explain the nature of power within the Empire. The British Empire from 1815 to 1914 will be viewed for the purposes of this book as a system of political control which was imposed by a strong (metropolitan) power, based in London, on a number of subordinate (peripheral) societies which were controlled directly by the agents of the British government and indirectly by locally elected governments, and whose foreign policy was dictated by the British government. It will be stressed that the nature of the power relationship between the British government and the people within the Empire differed from place to place.

It would probably take a historian several working lifetimes to master all the political, economic and social differences between the great variety of territories which made up the Empire between 1815 and 1914. It is enough, at this stage, for you to appreciate that the British, after 1815, operated one of the most flexible forms of imperialism ever seen in world history. The most significant differences in British rule will be examined in the chapters which follow, and will be described and commented upon. Rule within the Empire resembled a series of very different bi-lateral relationships between Britain and a varied collection of weaker states. At one end of the spectrum were areas such as Canada, Australia and New Zealand which, after 1870, were independent in all but name, and at the other extreme were places such as India and Kenya which remained under direct British rule in 1914 - and, in many cases, long afterwards.

b) Imperialism

The word 'imperialism' will be used frequently throughout the book, and it requires some explanation, despite the fact that it is a term in everyday use. Imperialism really explains the process of establishing rule and the nature of that rule within an empire. There have been many different definitions of imperialism. For example, it has been variously defined as 'the assertion of absolute force over others', 'an aggressive policy overseas', 'a form of tyranny which only differs in place and time', and 'the forcible exploitation by the strong of the weak'. However, it would be unwise to accept any one of these descriptions as a definition of British imperialism. The British saw their rule as essentially 'civilised' and beneficial to the people they governed, despite the fact that in many places it was viewed as a tyranny. Clearly, deciding exactly what was the nature of British rule largely depends on the point from which you are viewing. As a result, no one single definition of imperialism can be used to explain British rule in its totality.

Not surprisingly, given the emotive nature of imperial rule, historians have even found difficulty in agreeing on the best approach to analysing sources related to the Empire. The result is the development of three separate and often contradictory approaches. A 'top-down', metropolitan approach looks at sources located at the centre of imperial power and attempts to explain the motivations, policies and methods of the rulers. A 'bottom-up', peripheral approach examines sources from particular regions of the world which have come under British imperial rule. This approach looks at the problem from the perspective of the ruled and those British people, such as businessmen, 'men on the spot', and missionaries and traders, who were involved in imperialism outside the formal structures of the British government. A 'world-view', international relations approach sets the development of British imperialism within the broader and more general context of developments in the political and economic power structure of the international system of relations between nations. This approach uses evidence from both metropolitan and peripheral sources and develops theories about how power shifted within the world over centuries.

Each of the three approaches has its band of passionate supporters among historians. This means that the study of imperial history is one of the most contentious and controversial areas within the subject. Writers on imperialism cannot agree whether all imperial rule is essentially similar and is therefore capable of being explained by reference to a single theory, whether it is so diverse that it must be examined as a series of separate case-studies, or whether it is so broad that it can only be analysed successfully within an international context. For the student it is almost a matter of 'paying your money and taking your choice'. In the chapters that follow an attempt will be made to provide a 'survivor's guide' for students on this issue.

2 Empires from Earliest Times to 1500

There have been empires since the beginning of recorded history. The earliest known empire was in Mesopotamia (modern Iraq) in about 3000 BC. There were other empires at about the same time in Egypt, China, Persia, Mongolia, and India. In general, these ancient empires expanded by conquering defenceless people for some form of material or personal gain. The impulse of a society which is growing in power and influence to conquer, influence or dominate other groups of people is probably one of the oldest aspects of recorded human history.

The two most extensively researched ancient European empires are the 'classical' Empires of Greece and Rome. The Greek Empire came to prominence in the fifth century BC and was made up of two distinctly different types of political system. The Athenian Empire (based on the city state of Athens) operated a democratic constitution involving all its citizens (which did not include women and slaves), while the Spartan Empire (based on the city state of Sparta) was really an unequal military alliance, with one strong power dominating a number of much weaker ones.

a) The Greek Empire

Athens - as was the norm with ancient empires - built its empire by military conquest. The Athenian Empire established a uniform democratic constitution in which every citizen had a vote but in which Athens retained control of defence, domestic policy, and economic policy. The local people were taxed to support the defence and the administration of the Empire. Yet the rule of Athens was unstable, suffered frequent rebellions, and collapsed in less than 20 years.

The Spartans, who defeated the Athenians in the Peloponnesian War (431-404 BC), were the other major Greek empire-builders. They saw their empire as a partnership of equals. It was nothing of the sort. The Spartan Empire was little more than a military dictatorship ruled by a small tyrannical élite. It lasted less than 40 years. Aristotle in *The Politics* said of its fall, 'the Spartans always prevailed in war but were destroyed simply because they did not know how to use the leisure they had won, because they had practised no more fundamental skill than skill in war'. By 323 BC the Greek Empire had declined.

b) The Roman Empire

The Roman Empire - also built on military conquest - replaced the Greek Empire as the major ancient imperial power. Rome grew from a small group of villages in the third century BC into the largest, most powerful and most advanced empire of the ancient world. Although its population was never more than 4 million, the Roman Empire was probably the most remarkable empire there has ever been because it exercised greater control over its territories than any other power in recorded history.

Undoubtedly, the Romans had a fully-developed idea of imperialism. They set up uniform economic, political and social structures throughout their empire. They built cities wherever they went, encouraged art, education, and scholarship, introduced a single currency, employed customs officials and tax collectors, and built impressive monuments, roads, canals, public baths, vast sports arenas and much else. The Romans claimed they brought peace *(Pax Romanus)* to the areas they ruled and spread what they saw as a 'higher form of civilisation'. They used one derogatory word, 'barbarian', to describe all those who opposed their rule or remained outside their Empire.

Yet the Roman Empire declined. It changed from being a democratic republic into a dictatorship. The dictators, the army and the bureaucrats became an élite concerned with power for its own sake. They ignored public opinion and increased taxation in order to finance an orgy of extravagance and decadence. The rich were far richer and the poor far poorer at the end of the Empire than ever before. The Empire collapsed from the centre. The bureaucracy was a vast army of tax collectors protected by a vast army of soldiers. Taxation on the population increased year by year, and as taxation increased, productivity fell and apathy increased. The feeling that everyone was working for the benefit of a small élite became extremely powerful.

The central administration in Rome gradually broke down, the army split into factions, the people rioted on the streets, and Rome did, quite literally, burn. Yet, despite its miserable final years, we must not forget that the Empire, in its entirety, lasted well over 500 years. No power since that time has dominated for so long. The western European empire, based in Rome, was eventually defeated by the barbarian 'Huns' in the fifth century AD, but the Asian part of the Empire - known as the Byzantine Empire - survived until Constantinople (modern Istanbul) was captured by the Turks in 1453.

The contrast between the nature of these ancient empires and the British Empire is very marked. The British Empire was never a military dictatorship nor was it an alliance of equal partners. It was established partly by military conquest, but also significantly through the efforts of explorers and private individuals who set up small colonial settlements in Africa, India, North America and the Caribbean mainly for trading purposes.

The Roman army was generally regarded as a fearsome fighting force during the era of its dominance. The British army, on the other hand, frightened very few people. The British Empire depended primarily on naval power. This was used to defend the movement of goods on the high seas. As a consequence, the British ruled their Empire largely by bluff and diplomacy. They were never in the dominant or safe military position which the Romans had enjoyed. In addition, the Romans were famous for adapting well to local conditions and encouraging social mobility - a Spaniard once ruled the Roman Empire - whereas the British rulers remained aloof from the non-British and non-European people in their Empire. Whilst the Romans had very little problem with internal security, the British frequently faced riot and rebellion from the people they ruled. The British were defeated by the 13 American colonies in the War of Independence (1776-83) and faced major military conflicts or rebellions in Canada, India, the Sudan and South Africa between 1815 and 1914. The Empires of Athens and Rome taxed their colonies heavily and used the benefits of taxation in the imperial capital. The British never extracted taxation for use in the domestic economy from their colonies. Thus it can be seen that the 'classical' empires of Greece and Rome were very different entities from the British Empire.

3 The European Colonial Empires from 1500-1815

The British Empire grew up during the second major phase of European

Empire building which lasted from about 1500 to about 1815. This phase was inspired by the arrival of Christopher Columbus in 1492 in a place Europeans later called America. This 'discovery' - as it was when considered from a European point of view - of the 'New World' inspired a wave of European migration to America. Spain, Portugal, Holland, France and Britain all established empires on - for them - the other side of the Atlantic.

The European colonial empires which rose from 1500 onwards were run according to mercantilist principles. The aim of mercantilism, as practised by most European states, was to export more goods than were imported, thereby creating a profitable 'balance of trade' and increasing the wealth of the country, as judged by the amount of gold and silver held within it. It was believed that this process could be greatly assisted by securing supplies of highly prized commodities such as tea, sugar, coffee, spices, and other luxury goods from one's own colonies (thus avoiding the need for imports to the mother country and its territories), and by closing off the colonies to trade with other states (thereby restricting the market for their exports). Each of the five major European colonial powers used naval power to defend the trade routes between the mother country and its colonies, not only from rivals, but also from increasing numbers of pirates who roamed the high seas in search of riches.

The mercantilist system was thus maintained by strict limitations on the free flow of goods. There is little doubt that this was a system which protected vested interests in the metropolitan states, kept prices artificially high for the consumer because of the imposition of high import duties on foreign goods, and encouraged European powers to engage in costly naval wars and diplomatic feuds.

Although the general economic aims of the European overseas empires from 1500 to 1815 were similar, there were important differences in the forms of rule they adopted. Spain set the tone for European colonialism. The Spanish monarchy favoured a uniform system for the colonies it established in parts of South, Central and North America, the Caribbean and North Africa early in the sixteenth century. Catholicism, the Spanish language, Spanish laws, and Spanish customs were introduced wherever they ruled. But economics were also important. Huge amounts of gold and silver were shipped from Mexico and Peru between 1503 to 1660, thus stimulating considerable growth in Spanish trade in Europe. This encouraged other European states to seek treasure and riches through empire.

The Portuguese were the first European power to follow Spain to America in the sixteenth century by taking control of Brazil. Angola and Mozambique in Africa were also brought under Portuguese rule, and trading bases were established in India and the East Indies (modern Indonesia). But, unlike Spain, Portugal had no desire to introduce uniform principles throughout its empire. The colonies of the

Portuguese Empire were run as profit-making sugar, cotton and tobacco plantations, using slaves shipped from Africa. The Portuguese always put trade before the search for power and prestige, and by 1800 Brazil had become the world's leading sugar producer.

The Dutch also built an empire after 1600. It was run purely for trade and profit. The Dutch colonies in the East Indies, North America, and the Cape of Good Hope on the tip of southern Africa were ruled through the device of the private charter company. Such companies were given a Royal Charter by the Dutch monarchy which entitled them to rule the territories they had colonised. The Dutch Charter Companies froze out rivals by the use of naval power and they enforced a strict policy of protectionism to gain high profits. By 1815 the colonies in Africa and North America had been lost.

France also created a colonial empire in North America, India and the Caribbean. This empire was originally designed to 'augment the grandeur and glory of the King of France'. However, by the early-eighteenth century French colonial policy had become dominated by the drive for profit. The British and the French engaged in frenetic trade rivalry in America and India for most of the eighteenth century. On several occasions the competition escalated into open warfare. The most serious conflict was the Seven Years War of 1756-63. This led to the ending of French influence in India and in North America. The French Revolution of 1789 shattered the French monarchy, the Battle of Trafalgar (1805) shattered the French navy, and the Battle of Waterloo (1815) finally ended French dreams of dominating Europe. By 1815 France had lost all her colonies except a few small Caribbean islands.

4 The British Empire from 1500 to the Present Day

The development of the British Empire from 1500 to the present day went through three phases. The first phase was the era of the 'Old Colonial Empire' based on principles of mercantilism. This ran from early in the seventeenth century to the mid-Victorian period. The second era has become known as the 'Age of New Imperialism'. This lasted from about 1870 to 1914. This period was characterised by 'free trade', rapid British territorial expansion in Africa and Asia, and the resurgence of European imperial rivalry. The final phase has occupied the period from 1914 to the present day. This era saw the majority of the former territories of the Empire become a Commonwealth of independent nations bound only by bonds of friendship. The aim of this book is to explore three controvesial aspects of this story: the ending of the mercantilist period between 1815 and 1870, the expansion of the Empire in Africa and Asia between 1870 and 1914 and the impact of the Empire on British politics and society.

a) The Rise and Fall of the Old Colonial System

The British Empire grew after 1600 largely through the efforts of private individuals, private enterprise, and private trading companies. The first English chartered trading company was founded in 1555 to develop trade with Russia. Queen Elizabeth gave a charter to the East India Company in 1600 to develop trade with India. The Virginia Company, founded in 1606, established the first English colony in North America.

The year 1624 marks the first time the British government become directly involved in colonial affairs. James I brought the Virginia Company's settlements on the east coast of the present-day USA under direct British rule. Throughout the seventeenth century large numbers of explorers, traders and British settlers went to North America and the West Indies. By 1700 there were 13 British colonies on the east coast of North America with a population of 500,000 people. Contrary to popular myth, America was not the most profitable part of the old colonial Empire. That position was held by the West Indies because of its sugar crop. The vast sugar plantations of these picturesque Caribbean islands were worked by slaves shipped from west Africa. The British government spent enormous sums of money defending the West Indies from French, Spanish and Dutch ambitions throughout the eighteenth century.

In 1776 the growing British colonial empire in North America suffered a severe setback. The original 13 north American colonies (the colonies recently acquired from France did not join in) staged an armed rebellion. The Americans had come to believe that the restrictions of the mercantilist system were impeding their development. The colonists were successful in their rebellion and the outcome was the United States of America, a federal republic with a democratic constitution. Not surprisingly, the loss of the USA did much to discredit the idea of establishing colonial settlements of British people abroad. The result was a 'swing to the east', with a much greater emphasis on India in particular as a source of profitable trade and the development of Australia, which originally began life as a convict colony but which throughout the nineteenth century attracted over four million British settlers.

Between 1815 and 1870 the British had no serious imperial rivals. In this period the Old Colonial system was dismantled. Slavery was abolished, protectionism was ended, and self-government was granted to the remaining colonies of settlement (except the West Indies). This split the Empire into two distinct parts: the dependent empire (under direct rule) and the settlement empire (granted self-government).

b) The 'New Imperialism', 1870-1914

The second major phase of imperial expansion lasted from 1870 to 1914 and went hand in hand with the expansion of British industry, trade, and overseas investment. It also coincided with the resurgence of European imperial rivalry. The rapid growth of the British Empire took place mainly in Africa and Asia. The period also saw the British government take more of a lead in imperial affairs. The Empire became an important subject of discussion in British politics and influenced popular culture for the first time. The climax of all this imperial excitement was reached in the South African War of 1899-1902 (also known as the Boer War). This led to something of a loss of confidence in the idea of imperialism, although in economic terms the Empire continued to grow in importance as British industrial goods faced increasing competition, especially from the USA and Germany.

c) Empire to Commonwealth, 1914 to the Present Day

The third phase of British imperial rule saw the Empire transformed into a commonwealth of independent nations. After the First World War ideas of equality, mass democracy, and 'national self-determination' placed strains on the idea of imperialism. Between the two world wars Britain ended the occupation of Egypt, granted Eire independence, and promised self-government for India. The colonies of settlement (Australia, Canada, South Africa, and New Zealand) - known as 'dominions' - gained control over their foreign policies. The Balfour Declaration (1926) defined the dominions as 'autonomous communities within the British Empire'. The term Commonwealth - meaning a free association of friendly independent nations rather than an empire - came into general usage. Yet in the troubled 1930s the National Government gained acceptance for the concept of imperial preference, which made the Empire a market protected from foreign competition.

The Second World War placed enormous strains on Britain's defence of its empire, especially in the East. In the years after 1945 many people came to think of imperialism as incompatible with democratic government. The question became not would Britain grant independence to her colonies, but when. In 1947 India - the 'Jewel in the Crown' of the nineteenth-century Empire - was granted independence. Bit by bit between 1945 and 1970 independence was granted to all but a small handful of the territories of the Empire. The British government, the major political parties, and the British people hardly mourned the passing of the symbol of its former 'greatness'.

By 1973 Britain was a member of the European Economic Community (EEC). As the Empire dissolved the British government introduced stringent immigration controls to limit the number of people from former colonies who came to live in Britain. The ties of friendship between Britain and many of the former colonies still remains. The Commonwealth Games, attended by nearly all the former members of the Empire, is held every four years. The Commonwealth Conference, hosted by the Queen, remains a forum for political contact and discussion between the political leaders of the former colonies. The

Queen remains the head of state in many former colonies. But in recent times there has been a shrinkage of interest in the Commonwealth. For the majority of people in modern-day Britain the Empire has been forgotten almost as though it had never really existed.

5 The British Empire, 1815-1914, and the Historians

However, among historians the study of the Empire during its heyday between 1815 and 1914 remains a hot bed of controversy. There have been two general ways of explaining the development of British imperialism during this period - a conventional or traditional view and a revisionist interpretation.

The conventional way of looking at the British Empire between 1815 and 1914 has been to stress a clear divide between the period 1815-70, which has been viewed by traditionalists as 'an age of indifference' or 'an age of anti-imperialism', and the period 1870-1914, which has been thought of as an age of 'New Imperialism' and 'imperial excitement', supported by the British government which was serving the interests of 'finance capitalists' (J.A. Hobson) or 'monopoly capitalists' (Lenin). This discontinuity theory of British imperialism between 1815 and 1914 was a generally accepted view of the Empire until the 1950s.

The revisionists see matters differently. They claim that the British government did not really change its policy towards the Empire between 1815 and 1914. They suggest that the period 1815-70 was not 'an age of indifference' but was a period when British trade expanded rapidly in the 'formal' Empire of colonies and when a growing 'informal' world market for British goods and financial and shipping services was being brought into being. According to the revisionist view, the British government would have been happy for this 'imperialism of free trade' to continue into the indefinite future.

In this interpretation the actions of other European powers and instability in Africa and Asia were the prime reasons for British participation in the 'New Imperialism, which they engaged in as 'reluctant imperialists' rather than as active initiators, as the traditional view supposed. For example, Gallagher and Robinson, the leading revisionists, have argued that Britain participated in the Partition of Africa to protect British trading interests which were thought to be threatened by European rivals and African nationalism. This move, far from being something new, was no different, in essence, from the support the British government had always given to those trading overseas prior to 1815. The only real difference between the supposed 'age of indifference' and 'age of expansion' was the notable lack of threats to British interests from rivals between 1815 to 1870 and their obvious presence between 1870 and 1914.

It remains possible to find support for both the traditional and the revisionist interpretations of the British Empire between 1815 and 1914.

Yet today the majority of historians have more sympathy with the revisionist idea of continuity in the aims of British policy than with the notion of a sharp break in it sometime after 1870. The chapters that follow will explore the development of the Empire in the nineteenth century, bringing out the differences of interpretation between historians in the course of its analysis, before discussing the balance sheet of Empire in the concluding chapter.

Studying 'The British Empire, 1815-1914'

Readers will use this book for different purposes. A general reader may wish to read the whole volume from cover to cover. The student reader will probably use the book selectively to help with studies in courses on British History, Imperial History or European History. Many students will no doubt concentrate on the topics related to popular areas such as the Partition of Africa, the Indian Mutiny, and the roles of Disraeli, Gladstone and Joseph Chamberlain. The contents section, the chronological table and the index should make it possible to locate the sections dealing with these areas quickly. The study guides at the end of each chapter are designed to help you plan your work on each of the topics covered by the book.

There will be many readers who will use the book as the first step in studying the subject in considerable depth. It needs to be appreciated that the study of British imperialism is extremely emotive. This makes impartiality for historians who write on the subject all the more difficult. Imperial history is really the story of how a group of more powerful people rule a group of less powerful people - often against their will. You will find that bias caused by subjectivity, which is present in most historical areas, is even more prominent in the study of imperialism. This is epecially true in this post-imperial age when British historians are faced with historians of the former colonies writing their own interpretations of British rule which often challenge British and Euro-centric myths.

To study imperial history successfully, especially in a post-imperial age and within the context of a multi-ethnic and multi-cultural society, requires a willingness to appreciate all sides in the debate - especially the British or Euro-centric position, and the interpretations of historians who think of themselves as victims of British rule. It is important to accept that there is no one 'right' way to approach the study of the British Empire. Of necessity, what follows will have been written from one point of view and will be based on one set of values and expectations. The serious student should make a conscious effort to identify what these are, and in his or her subsequent reading should endeavour to consider the ideas of writers who start from a different position. Only in that way will the reader be well placed to form balanced views about this highly emotive topic.

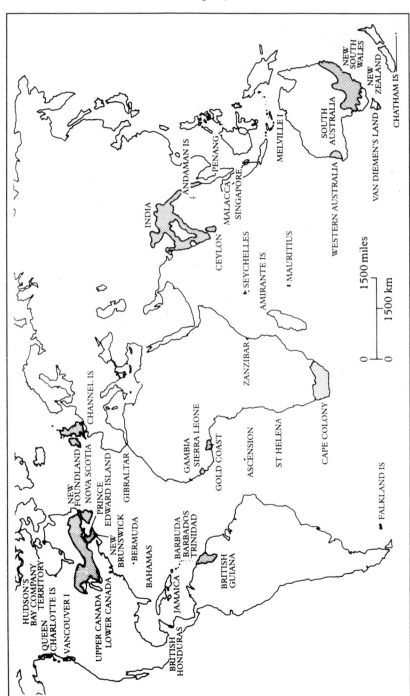

The British Empire in 1837

CHAPTER 2

An Age of Indifference?
The British Empire, 1815-70

1 The British Empire in 1815

The British Empire in 1815 was hardly a uniform association. It had no single constitution, religion, language or system of law. The colonies of the Empire had very little in common with each other except their link with Britain. There was wide variation in the forms of rule. For example, India was ruled by a private charter company, Ascension Island by a Captain in the Royal Navy, and Canada by an all-powerful Governor appointed by the British government.

The major decisions regarding the Empire were taken by the Colonial Office. This small sub-branch of the War Office was located in a house at the end of Downing Street. It was not until 1854 that colonial affairs were given a separate government department with its own Secretary of State. The British government was normally too concerned with domestic politics to play a leading role in colonial affairs. As a result, a major colonial crisis might only lead to a poorly attended parliamentary debate. Sometimes a select committee of MPs or a government inquiry was set up to investigate a major issue. Apathy was the normal state of affairs. The government was quite happy to leave the day-to-day management of the Empire to the officials in the Colonial Office. In its turn, the Colonial Office was quite content to leave responsibility for the routine running of colonies with administrators in the colonies themselves.

Only in matters concerning trade did the British government have a coherent policy in 1815. This was mercantilism. A wide range of laws underpinned the mercantilist system. The Navigation Acts ensured that all of a colony's imports and exports were carried by British ships. British goods were given a monopoly in colonial markets. The colonies were only allowed to export goods not produced in Britain. Protective tariffs were used to freeze out foreign goods. There is no doubt that the colonies of the British Empire existed primarily for the benefit of the British economy, at the expense of their own social, economic and political development.

The colonies themselves were divided into two broad categories: the colonies of settlement and the 'dependent' or 'crown' colonies. The colonies of settlement (West Indies, Canada, Cape Colony, Australia) were founded exclusively by people of British or European origin. They were governed by a British-appointed governor, permanent British officials, and small - virtually powerless - local councils. This was all they had in common. Canada had a large group of French speakers; Cape Colony was dominated by Dutch settlers; 90 per cent of the population of the West Indies were African slaves; Australia was really an enormous jail for British convicts.

Outside the areas of British settlement stood the 'dependent' or 'crown' colonies. They had come into existence for a variety of reasons: mainly because they could act as trading or naval bases (most ships needed to be revitualled or repaired frequently). They had few British or European settlers and were ruled by small groups of British officials who possessed autocratic power. The exception was India, the largest dependent colony of all. The sheer size of this vast sub-continent (even though much of it was not under British control in 1815) placed it in a special category all of its own. A Governor-General, working in association with the privately-owned East India Company, ruled it until 1858. Afterwards power over India was shared between a Viceroy, the India Office, a Secretary of State and a Council for India.

The other dependencies made up a hotchpotch of coastal ports and islands. A few coastal areas on the west and southern coastlines of Africa were under British rule as well as a large variety of strategically-placed islands - such as Malta, and Mauritius - scattered around the oceans of the world. They were used variously as naval bases, suppliers of food and raw materials, and trading stations.

This disparate Empire served three important functions. Firstly, it conferred great-power status on Britain as the world's major colonial power. Secondly, the Empire provided Britain with reliable sources of food and raw materials and a captive market for British exports. This was important because Britain was unable to feed and employ its population without imports of food and raw materials from abroad. The country imported 31 per cent of its food and 61 per cent of its raw materials in 1815. Thirdly, the Empire provided the Royal Navy with a large number of important naval bases from which it was able to dominate the sea lanes of the world.

Britain's imperial dominance coincided with her economy's dramatic expansion to leading world status. This had been made possible not so much by the strange collection of colonies described above as by the development of her industries and her banking services, and the accumulation of capital within the domestic economy which had been gathering pace since 1750. After 1815 British economic influence spread throughout the world and ensured that Britain was to be the leading economic force in first half of the nineteenth century. Such a dramatic change in the fortunes of the British economy (it is known as the Industrial Revolution) was bound to have an important impact on the old colonial system.

2 The Changing Empire

As a consequence of Britain's economic expansion there were important changes within the Empire between 1815 and 1870. It might be thought that because the amount of territory controlled by Britain increased by an average of about 100,000 square miles per year during this period the emphasis was on extending the Empire's size. In fact, this was not the case. Strange as it may seem, this huge increase in the extent of the Empire was not the result of a co-ordinated policy of conquest by the British government. The new territories acquired came under British rule largely because a number of unconnected local circumstances. In many cases new territories were acquired 'defensively' - to protect areas already under British control, to safeguard trading interests that had come under threat, or to come to the assistance of British nationals in the area. Certainly there was little attempt made to establish settlement colonies as had been the practice in the seventeenth and eighteenth centuries. The only exception was New Zealand, where a number of private interests contrived to force the government's hand.

In the period up to 1870 the majority of British industrialists and traders who were involved in import and export had their eyes set on a world rather than an imperial market. As it transpired, trade outside the Empire was increasing far more rapidly than trade within the Empire. By 1860 only 25 per cent of total British trade was with the Empire. The major new fields of British investment that were being opened up outside the Empire were in the USA, Latin America - especially Argentina and the Far East. This led to a shift in attitudes towards the future of the Empire. Increasingly, questions were raised in Britain about the need to maintain the Old Colonial System which, it was argued, had outlived its usefulness. A movement of free traders viewed the mercantilist system as out of step with the trend of the times. It was against this background that significant changes to British imperial rule were brought about between 1815 and 1870. The most important social reform was the abolition of slavery. The major political change was the granting of responsible self-government to the settlement colonies. The major economic reform was the abandonment of protectionism.

a) Social Reform: The Abolition of Slavery

The continued use of slave labour in British colonies was the first point of attack. Slave labour had not only been a leading feature of British imperialism but of all the major imperial powers until the nineteenth century. The British had used slaves in North America since the seventeenth century. The system operated in the following way. African slaves were sold to British slave traders in West African ports. They were transported across the Atlantic by ship in horrific conditions and then sold in the West Indies or North America at auction to the highest bidder (see the poster on page 16). Between 18 and 25 million people were forced to leave Africa in this way during the era of legalised slavery.

The injustice of slavery was under attack by the late-eighteenth century. Humanitarian reformers, church missionary societies, and radical writers formed an effective anti-slavery pressure group, led by William Wilberforce, a Tory MP. The British government soon bowed to this pressure and introduced several measures designed to end the slave trade. The trading of slaves by British citizens in Africa was made illegal in 1807. In an attempt to prevent foreign slavers taking over where the British had left off, the movement of slaves on the high seas was made an offence in maritime law in 1811. The Royal Navy was used in a fairly successful campaign to prevent other nations transporting slaves across the Atlantic. In 1819 a register of all existing slaves was drawn up by Britain so that any illegal additions could subsequently be traced. By the 1820s most European powers had outlawed the slave trade. Support for the Anti-Slavery Society grew. In 1830 2,600 anti-slavery petitions were presented to parliament. In 1831 there was

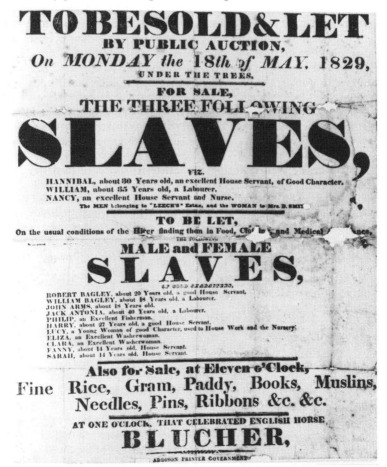

A slavery poster from the West Indies (1829)

an unsuccessful uprising by slaves in Jamaica which resulted in 500 deaths.

By this stage the Whig government hardly needed much convincing of the need to introduce an anti-slavery act. The major opponents of abolition were, not surprisingly, the slave owners who were mainly sugar merchants and plantation owners in the West Indies. They demanded substantial compensation to the tune of £30 million. They finally agreed to accept £18,669,401. This was an enormous sum, representing £38 per slave. The Abolition of Slavery Act became law in August 1834. It stipulated that all slaves under six years of age should be freed immediately. The rest were to remain part-slave, part-free until 1838.

The abolition of slavery was portrayed by the Whig government - and a large majority of British historians - as a genuine humanitarian reform. The Colonial Office said it was part of a general desire to 'transfer to distant regions the greatest possible amount of civil liberty and the forms of social order for which Britain is deeply indebted for the rank she holds among civilisation'.

The news was not greeted with satisfaction everywhere. The Boers - ruggedly independent Dutchmen - in Cape Colony on the tip of southern Africa were outraged at the decision and refused to accept it. Many of them left the Cape and journeyed northwards into the interior of southern Africa on a 'Great Trek' in search of land that was outside of British control. By 1860 the independent Boer republics of the Orange Free State and the Transvaal had been established.

The historical debate over the abolition of slavery has produced a great deal of controversy. Much of the work of British historians has laid emphasis on the pressure-group activities of the anti-slavery movement which, they claim, created a climate of opinion in British government circles which led directly to abolition. The evidence of the anti-slavery movement, parliamentary debates and the private papers of important members of the Whig government supports this view. West Indian historians, on the other hand, have countered by showing that economic self-interest played its part as well. They have looked at economic data which shows that, although in the eighteenth century West Indian sugar was a one-way ticket to economic prosperity, it was fighting a losing battle against foreign competition by the early years of the nineteenth century. Many British sugar producers were losing money in the years which led up to abolition. The compensation offered by the British government gave the slave owners an easy way to escape from what was already looking like a bleak economic future.

This difference of opinion over the motives surrounding the abolition of slavery between British and West Indian historians seems unlikely to be resolved. It illustrates one of the main difficulties of imperial history. The historians of the imperialist power - in this case Britain - have tended to portray the actions of their native country in the best possible light. The sources available come from the rulers, not the ruled, and support this interpretation. Yet historians of ex-colonies have claimed that this evidence does not tell the whole story and that it distorts the underlying economic context in which abolition occured. The falling profits within the sugar companies and among plantation owners was for West Indian historians 'the hidden agenda' which underpinned abolition. This trend among historians of the ex-colonies to question the assumptions of older interpretations written by British historians has become known as 'the Empire striking back', and attempting to expose the underlying economic motives which often guided the actions of the their former rulers.

How do we resolve this emotive debate? It is not easy. It seems 'logical', (a concept beloved of Europeans) to suppose that if slavery was barbaric, degrading and inhuman, abolishing it must have been the act of enlightened and progressive people. This allows the British to see themselves as the 'good imperialists'. They sleep easy. But West Indian historians have asked what the British 'humanitarians' did for the ex-slaves once they were freed. The abolition of slavery, by any 'objective' (another favourite European concept) assessment, was a disaster for the West Indian economy. Once slavery had been abolished British investment drained away. The abolition in 1852 of the duty on sugar brought into Britain from outside the Empire was a serious blow to the West Indian sugar industry from which it never fully recovered. The West Indies - 'Jewel in the Crown' of old Colonial Empire - became an economic backwater. The British government did nothing to improve the lives of the former slaves. In fact, the West Indies, the oldest settlement colony of all, was defined as part of the dependent empire after abolition, and was denied self-government. The visible chains of slavery were replaced by invisible chains of poverty, poor education, deprivation, and racial prejudice.

b) Political Reform: The Development of Self-government

An equally far-reaching reform took place in the political organisation of the Empire between 1815 and 1870. This was the development of self-government for the colonies of settlement. This was the most important political reform to take place within the Empire during the whole of the nineteenth century.

It came about in a rather haphazard fashion. The starting point was an armed rebellion in Canada in December 1837. The main cause of the Canadian rebellion was the arbitrary rule of the British Governor and his permanent officials who had persistently ignored the wishes of locally elected councils for greater democracy, and had turned the French settlers of Lower Canada into an oppressed minority. The rebellion was really the culmination of years of discontent with British colonial government in Canada. It was easily put down by British troops. Lord Durham, a Whig, was sent to Canada to investigate the causes of the rebellion. The Durham Report (1839) squarely placed the blame on the British administration which was termed 'irresponsible government'. Durham recommended uniting Upper and Lower Canada to form a single province with a truly representative system of government. The idea was for Britain to retain overall control but to allow a locally elected government to decide domestic policy.

The Durham Report was a 'revolutionary' document in that it became the blueprint for the introduction of self-government to most of the other colonies of settlement. Canada led the way. Upper and Lower Canada were united in 1840. A National Federal Assembly was created for the whole of Canada, and the individual provinces were given control over internal affairs. By 1867 Canada was a fully functioning self-governing colony with a democratic voting system and its own domestic policy.

By the mid-Victorian period the British government was prepared to grant responsible self-government to all 'politically advanced colonies'. In practice this meant well-established colonies with substantial British and European populations. If a colony was poor with a large non-European population then it did not qualify. Such colonies were treated like children dependent on the mother country. Therefore, self-government was confined to the 'white colonies'. New Zealand in 1856 and Cape Colony in 1872 were granted democratic self-government with free elections. The Australian colonies of New South Wales, Victoria, Southern Australia were granted self government in 1855, Queensland was given it in 1859. The only aspect of policy over which Britain retained control was foreign relations.

These self-governing colonies were a unique new development in the history of the Empire. They represent a genuine devolution of political power. The Canadian rebellion was the catalyst for the change. Yet it was the British government which masterminded it and extended it. It was once traditional for historians to interpret the granting of self-government as indicative of a desire on the part of the British government to break up the Empire. In more recent studies this view has been called into question. It is difficult to show a link between the granting of self-government and a broader desire to abandon the Empire. It is equally difficult to show any 'grass roots' desire within the colonies for independence. Indeed, if Cain and Hopkins in *British Imperialism* (1993) are correct, then in economic terms, the colonies of settlement became much more dependent on British investment and British defence after they were granted self-government. The idea that the introduction of self-government implied the imminent break up of the Empire is generally greeted with scepticism among modern-day historians.

c) Economic Reform: The Triumph of Free Trade

Yet it is the causes and the effects of the introduction of free trade by the British government between 1846 and 1860 which has created the greatest interest among historians attempting to explain the signficance of this period for the development of British imperialism. The introduction of free trade grew from changes in the domestic economy, the most important being the enormous lead Britain had gained over other economic rivals in industry, trade, and finance during the first half of the nineteenth century. An appreciation of the impact of industrialisation on British finance, society and government policy is crucial to any understanding of British history since 1815.

The British economy had been developing impressively in the late-eighteenth century. After 1815 the pace of industrial expansion was even more remarkable. In the period 1815-60 Britain was responsible for 60 per cent of the total growth of world manufacturing. In 1850 Britain accounted for 50 per cent of world trade in coal, cotton, and iron. A third of all overseas trade was carried out by British ships. In 1850 Britain's Gross National Product (GNP) - the value of all goods and services produced - was higher than that of China and Russia combined.

There were other important developments. The British population grew from 9 million in 1801 to 18 million in 1851 and reached 36 million by 1901. Large cities mushroomed, and railways transformed internal transport. The steamship and the telegraph transformed worldwide communications. A whole new international banking and finance system based in London spread its tentacles around the world. One illustration of this influence was a growth of British capital investment abroad. A recent 'guesstimate' has suggested an increase from £30 million in 1851 to £70 million in 1871. Other figures have shown more dramatic increases. The exact rate of the growth of British investment abroad has proved notoriously difficult for economic historians to calculate. Nevertheless, it appears clear that the trend was upward during the whole of the nineteenth century. The income derived from overseas investment created a further surplus of capital which spawned the development of other nations. The steady expansion of the British economy was achieved with only 2 per cent of the world's total population.

Not surprisingly, industrialisation influenced groups outside parliament to fight for political and economic reform. Yet change came slowly. This was due to the dominance of the landed aristocracy over the British political system. Any suggestion of reform met with resistance from landed interests at Westminster. Extra-parliamentary pressure became the primary means of influencing the government to implement reform. There were three main sources of extra-parliamentary pressure on the British government to introduce free trade. The first was the

Anti-Corn Law League. This was set up in 1839 and was the political voice of Manchester industrial free-trade radicalism. The second influential group was made up of free-trade economists. The writings of Adam Smith, David Ricardo, James Mill and others laid out the probable benefits of free trade for the British economy. This added intellectual weight to the movement. The third group was made up of bankers and financiers in the City of London. This group of 'gentlemanly capitalists' was a rising force within British society and exerted a growing influence over the British government.

Slowly but surely the ideas of all three groups penetrated government economic policy. The first moves came in the 1820s. William Huskisson, President of the Board of Trade (1824-7), allowed foreign countries to trade with colonies, lowered duties on a large number of imports and relaxed shipping regulations to allow foreign ships into British and colonial ports. During the 1830s the Whig government continued this general trend of relaxing trade restrictions. Yet it was a Conservative - Sir Robert Peel, the son of a Lancashire cotton mill owner and Prime Minister, 1841-6 - who made the most dramatic attacks on protectionism. The free trade budgets of 1842 and 1845 reduced duties on a wide range of imported goods. A more remarkable move was the abolition of the protective tariff on imported corn - known as the repeal of the Corn Laws - in 1846. This shattered the confidence of the landowning élite and the unity of the Conservative Party, and led to the fall of Peel. But it failed to halt the march towards free trade. In 1849 the Navigation Acts - which were designed to give Britain a monopoly of the transport of goods to the colonies - were repealed. In 1852 Benjamin Disraeli, the bitterest critic of Peel in 1846, said that nothing remained of protectionism except 'rags and tatters'. The free trade budgets of William Gladstone in the 1850s and 1860s removed all the remaining tariffs on imported goods.

The triumph of free-trade ideas meant that the Old Colonial system was dead. The protection of colonial markets from foreign competition had been central to that system. Free trade ended the commercial monopoly Britain had enjoyed over her colonial markets for centuries. After 1850 the British Empire was being defended at great cost to the British taxpayer even though it offered the mother country no exclusive economic benefits.

The colonies of the dependent empire were mainly losers from the free trade revolution. India was the biggest loser of all. Because it was denied self-government, it could not impose a protective tariff to save its own domestic industry from a flood of British imports. The Indian cotton industry was destroyed by free trade. The same applied to many crafts and trades throughout the other colonies of the dependent empire. On the other hand, the settlement colonies were winners from the introduction of free trade. The granting of self-government allowed them to impose tariffs on British goods, to attract investment, and to sell their own goods in the tariff-free and open British market. This made the self-governing colonies undoubted winners in the new free-trading economic order of the British Empire.

3 The Historical Debate

A large number of writers and historians have suggested that the advent of free trade led to a period of indifference towards the Empire in mid-Victorian society. Lenin claimed in his *Imperialism: The Highest Stage of Capitalism* (1916) that, 'when free trade competition was at its height between 1840 and 1860 the leading British politicians were of the opinion that the complete independence of the British colonies was not only inevitable but desirable'. The idea of 'mid-Victorian indifference' towards the Empire was an agreed interpretation among historians until the 1950s.

There is plenty of contemporary evidence to support the case for 'indifference' in the mid-Victorian period. For example, Richard Cobden (one of the leaders of the Anti-Corn Law League) argued that the colonies were a burden on the taxpayer and should be granted independence. The *Edinburgh Review* remarked of the colonies in 1851: 'the very object to which we founded, governed, defended and cherished them has been abandoned: why should we any longer incur the cost?' In 1849 Lord Grey, the Colonial Secretary, expressed the opinion that a wide range of people in the 'highest quarters' in the British ruling élite had no interest in preserving the Empire. A number of government actions in the mid-Victorian period also support the conventional view. In the 1860s there were British troop withdrawals from New Zealand, Canada, and Australia. In 1865 a Parliamentary Select Committee recommended the abandonment of British possessions in West Africa. The granting of self-government was extended to all the colonies of settlement except Western Australia and its Northern territories and the West Indies.

Yet ever since the publication of a famous article entitled 'The Imperialism of Free Trade' by J.A. Gallagher and R. Robinson in 1953 the old orthodox interpretation has come under sustained attack. Gallagher and Robinson claimed that the traditional view concentrated too heavily on the speeches, writings and letters of a small group of free-trade liberals who had little influence over government policy, the Colonial Office, or the two major political parties. They also maintained that the existing orthodoxy failed to explain why the Empire expanded so rapidly between 1815 and 1870, and especially after 1841. This was the period during which Britain annexed or occupied New Zealand, the Gold Coast, Hong Kong, Natal, Lauban, Lagos, Sierra Leone, Lower Burma, Kowloon, Basutoland, the Transvaal, and Berar.

Gallagher and Robinson asked why all these imperial adventures continued if the will of government and of intellectual and public opinion had turned against them. On closer inspection they found the age of indifference to be a historical myth. It was just as easy to portray the period from 1815 to 1870 as an 'age of expansion'. They suggested that there were really two Empires developing side by side after 1815. There was a 'formal' Empire of colonies Britain controlled directly in order to maintain commercial supremacy, and an 'informal' Empire where Britain was content to relax outright control as long as no threat existed to disrupt British trading interests. They claimed that the move towards a 'formal' and an 'informal' Empire was primarily driven by the economic dominance of British industry, trade, and finance, and that after 1815 governments acted on the principle of 'trade with informal control if possible, trade with rule where necessary'.

At first historians were sceptical about the views of Gallagher and Robinson. The idea of 'formal' and 'informal' Empire seemed to exist more in the the minds of the authors than in the actual records of the British government. Oliver MacDonagh, a recognised expert on nineteenth-century British government, argued that there was no significant evidence of a planned attempt to dominate markets systematically by informal means in the period after 1815. The early critics of Gallagher and Robinson tended to treat their views as a clever theory about the world economy which bore little relation to the actions of the British government itself.

Yet Gallagher and Robinson's distinction between 'formal' and 'informal' methods of imperial rule is now at the forefront of modern studies of British imperialism. The work of economic historians - now computer enhanced - is increasingly revealing that the British government in the nineteenth century was often led into action by economic forces beyond their control. There are few historians these days who would rely exclusively on evidence from government records or on the speeches and writings - often quoted out of context - of free-trade liberals.

The prevailing emphasis within the modern debate on British imperialism is the need to look at developments in the nineteenth century within an international framework. It appears from recent research by economic historians that the British government, traders and financiers did prefer informal control to outright rule. After 1815 Britain was looking for new markets, new areas for profitable investment, and stable sources of raw materials as much as for new places to plant a British flag. The idea that Britain was attempting to gain a dominant position within a worldwide trade and finance system in the years following Waterloo has a growing army of well-informed supporters. The workings of 'gentlemanly capitalists' in the City of London is being given far more detailed scrutiny than the policy of the British government. The general trend in recent studies has been to stress the importance of economic factors within financial sectors of Britain and the world economy in leading a process which the government ultimately accepted, and eventually championed. It is increasingly important in the current debate to stress that profitable trade and investment with countries around the world was becoming as important to Britain as the colonies of the Empire itself.

4 Conclusion

The period 1815-70 saw the principles which had guided the old colonial system since the days of Oliver Cromwell in the seventeenth century swept away. Slavery was abolished, direct rule was replaced by responsible self-government everywhere except for two Australian provinces and the West Indies, the Navigation Acts were repealed, and free trade was introduced.

A central issue which has fascinated historians writing on the period has been the question whether the end of mercantilism was followed by widespread indifference to the future of the Empire. The debate has concentrated on a discussion of which facts are the significant ones. It has been suggested that the traditional view of 'an age of indifference' relied on the wrong facts gleaned from unrepresentative contemporary public figures - most of whom supported free trade. The revisionists have produced facts relating to trade and territorial expansion which show a different picture. However, it is still a matter of dispute whether the 'guesstimates' on British overseas investment of economic historians are any more reliable than the evidence of mid-Victorian attitudes previously put forward.

The idea that an 'informal' British Empire was being put in place during this period must also be treated with great caution. It appears the critics of Gallagher and Robinson do seem to have a fair point when they suggest it is not accurate to call areas which were under no form of British government control or domination an 'informal' Empire. Britain was the major trading partner of the USA in this period but its direct or informal influence over the American government was limited. The British also held a dominant trading position with Argentina and yet had very little influence over the Argentine government. The idea of an 'informal' empire still remains a clever idea which does not seem always to 'fit the facts'.

However, Gallagher and Robinson are on firmer ground when they suggest the British government did not seriously consider independence for the settlement colonies. On balance, it is probably correct to view the social, economic and political reforms enacted by the British government towards the Empire as part of an exercise to strengthen rather than to weaken the Empire. In official circles the prevailing view was that imperial reform was designed to build a 'new' Empire of settlement colonies granted greater freedom and self-government and a dependent empire whose people were being 'educated in the arts of government' so that they too could one day - even if a very long time into the future - become self-governing colonies of the Empire.

More recently, British historians have begun to attack the traditional view that these decades should be portrayed as 'an Age of Reform' in British policy towards the Empire. A great deal of time and energy is now being devoted to showing that reform was enacted but 'nothing really changed'. It has been argued that slavery was replaced by other forms of bonded labour and the exploitation of Asian and later African workers. The granting of responsible government is now more generally viewed as a tactic to save money on the growing British defence budget than as part of a grand design to break up the Empire. The link between industrial growth and imperial trade has been shown to have been somewhat exaggerated. As C.A. Bayly in *Imperial Meridan: The British Empire and the World 1780-1831* (1989) puts it: 'the old construct of an age of reform ... was obviously too simplistic'. The reforms which were enacted came about in a 'piecemeal and often confused' fashion. The period 1815 to 1870 is now more broadly viewed by historians as a period when new forms of imperial power, new networks of control and when new partnerships between metropole and periphery were being constructed. As a result notions such as 'age of reform' and 'age of indifference' are now viewed as an oversimplified means of examining an extremely complex set of changes.

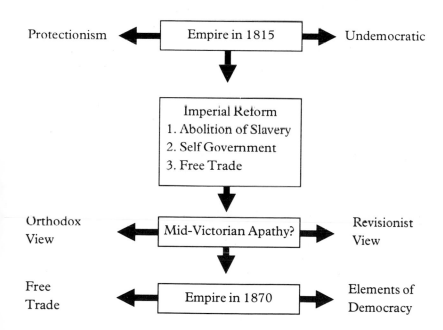

Summary - The British Empire, 1815-70

Making Notes on 'The British Empire, 1815-70'

This chapter has focused on the impact of imperial reform in the period 1815 to 1870. The simplest way to make notes would be to use the headings and sub-headings to provide a framework for a detailed summary of the main points in each section. If you make your notes this way, please remember to cross reference this chapter with the chapter on the Empire in Asia between 1815 and 1870 as it provides useful evidence of developments in India and of the 'open-door' policy in China.

A more challenging (because you have to think more) and potentially more useful way of making notes would be to follow the plan given below.

1 The Nature of the Empire. Draw up definitions of the following terms: mercantilism; settlement colony; dependent colony.
2 The Abolition of Slavery. Describe the contrasting views of British and West Indian historians.
3 Responsible Government. Explain the causes and consequences of the Canadian rebellion, and the reasons why responsible government was confined to the settlement colonies.
4 Free Trade. Explain the ways in which the introduction of free trade was a significant change in the economic policy of the Empire. Which colonies gained and which lost from free trade?
5 The Historical Debate. Describe the arguments used by both sides of the Gallagher and Robinson controversy over 'indifference'. Define 'formal' and 'informal' Empire.
6 India and the Far East. Remember to take notes from chapter 4, especially on British rule in India. Is this evidence of indifference? Was the 'open-door' policy in China an example of 'informal' imperialism?

Answering essay questions on 'The British Empire, 1815-70'

Not surprisingly, the emphasis on questions set in this period is on imperial reform. Study the following examples:

1 To what extent was the British Empire transformed in the period 1815 to 1870?
2 Did the coming of free trade lead to mid-Victorian indifference towards the Empire?
3 What part was played by economic factors in stimulating imperial reform between 1815 and 1870?
4 Identify and explain the major social, economic and political reforms in the British Empire between 1815 and 1870.

5   Consider the view that 'imperial reform in the period from 1815 to 1870 was confined to the colonies of settlement'.

6   In what ways did the Empire of 1870 differ from the Empire in 1815?

Identify the questions you feel confident about answering and those which you feel are beyond you. Then ask yourself why you feel as you do. Could it be because the notes you have made are inadequate?

The wording of question 4 needs to be read carefully. The question asks you both to 'identify' and to 'explain'. A good idea would be to draw up a list of all the imperial reforms in this period and then to attempt to explain their significance in your own words. This could then be used as the basis of an essay plan for the question.

Questions 1 and 6 appear to be very similar but, in fact, they require very different approaches. The answer to one of these questions should contain a significant amount of information about what did not change as well as a full explanation of the major developments that took place. Which question requires this approach?

A strong opening to your essay will attract the eye of even an overworked essay marker no matter which of the questions you attempt. It is worth spending time thinking of a striking phrase or an interesting idea to include in your first sentence. Of course, a good beginning is never more than 'the icing on the cake', but if it is done well it can influence the examiner's attitude towards the rest of your essay. Sometimes this can pay handsome dividends.

Source-based questions on 'The British Empire, 1815-70'

1 The Portrayal of Slavery
Carefully study the illustration of the slavery poster (page 16) and answer the following questions.
a)   Briefly explain what the poster depicts. (3 marks)
b)   Of what value is the poster as a historical source? (3 marks)
c)   What does the poster reveal about the probable attitudes of slave owners? (4 marks)
d)   In what ways were such advertisements likely to have contributed to the growth of an anti-slavery movement? (5 marks)

CHAPTER 3

The Partition of Africa

In the late-nineteenth century a small group of European powers suddenly and dramatically became involved in a territorial Partition of Africa. Between 1880 and 1900 90 per cent of the territory of Africa was appropriated by a handful of European powers (see the map on page 45). Britain acquired nearly 5 million square miles of land, France gained 3.5 million and Germany, Belguim and Italy shared 2.5 million between them.

The 'Scramble for Africa' (as it was popularly termed) has been the subject of intense debate among historians ever since. In order to develop an understanding of this many-faceted topic it is necessary to build up a sound knowledge of the main events and of the different interpretations that have been advanced to explain them. It is also important to reach a conclusion about the reasons why each of the European powers (including Britain) became involved. To help in this task the chapter has been divided into three sections. The first looks at Britain's role in the major events of the Partition, the second explores the different interpretations of its causes, and the third offers an assessment of the reasons why each of the European powers took part.

1 Britain and the Partition of Africa

Before the Partition Britain's involvement in Africa was on a relatively small scale. She had no colonies at all in North or East Africa. In West Africa she controlled no more than several small coastal areas - Gambia, Sierra Leone (a free slave colony), Gold Coast Castle, and Lagos. In South Africa there was rather more of a presence: Cape Colony and Natal were formal colonies, and Britain claimed the right to control the foreign relations of the two 'Boer' republics, the Orange Free State and Transvaal. But this strong position was not seen as a spring-board for further acquisition, and in 1880 there were no plans to extend the British Empire in Africa. On the contrary, Gladstone, the Prime Minister, was committed to a policy of 'non-intervention' in colonial affairs. Yet in 1882 in a startling *volte face* he ordered the occupation of Egypt. This turned out to be the starting point of the Partition of Africa.

a) North Africa: The Occupation and Defence of Egypt

The Turkish (Ottoman) Empire had captured Egypt in 1517 and thereafter had expanded along the North African coast to Tripoli, Tunis, Algeria and Morocco. But by the late-nineteenth century the Ottoman Empire was in decline. This worried the British government

which feared that Ottoman possessions in North Africa would fall into
the hands of rival European powers and thereby threaten British
interests in the area. Lord Palmerston summed up British policy
towards Egypt in 1860: 'we do not want to have Egypt. What we wish
about Egypt is that it should be attached to the Turkish Empire, which is
security against it belonging to another European power. We wish to
trade with Egypt and travel through Egypt.'

The French took a different view. They encouraged Egypt to break
away from the Ottoman Empire and French investors poured money
into the country after 1850. The most dramatic example of French
investment was a bold plan to construct the Suez Canal, which opened
in 1869. It connected the Mediterranean with the Red Sea. It was
designed by a Frenchman (Ferdinand de Lesseps), and built by tens of
thousands of Egyptian labourers under the supervision of French
engineers.

The completion of the Suez Canal led to a large influx of British
investment. British banks offered the Egyptian government enormous
loans which were used for economic development. Alexandria became a
major port, over 1,000 miles of railway track were laid, arms were
bought, and schools, roads and public buildings were built. Between
1863 and 1879 Egypt's foreign debt increased from £3 million to £100
million. The interest rate to be paid on it leapt in the same period from 7
per cent to 20 per cent. By 1875 Egypt had a 'debt crisis' which seemed
likely to lead to the country's economic collapse. Although he still owed
allegiance to the Sultan of Turkey, Ismail, the Egyptian ruler, in
desperation requested the British and French governments to provide
expert economic advice.

The British sent Stephen Cave, a British Treasury official, to
investigate the financial state of Egypt. Cave believed Egypt's economic
problems had two major causes.

1 She suffers from the ignorance, dishonesty, waste and extravagance of the East, such as have brought her Suzerien [the Sultan
  of Turkey] to the verge of ruin, and at the same time from the vast
  expense caused by hasty and inconsiderate endeavours to adapt to
5 civilisation.

Cave's report blamed Egypt's economic crisis on poor economic
management and the swift rise in interest rates but concluded that,

1 the resources of Egypt are sufficient, if properly managed, to meet
  her liabilities, but as all her available assets are pledged for the
  charges of existing loans, some fresh combination is necessary in
  order to fund at a moderate rate the present onerous floating debt
5 ... A body of high class Europeans ... men like our Indian officials
  should take over the task of running the Egyptian economy.

In 1878 an Anglo-French rescue plan emerged. This was based on the ideas put forward in the Cave Report. The plan was simple. French government officials and British financial experts would take control of the Egyptian economy. The French would look after government expenditure; the British would raise revenue. This 'dual economic control' began in 1878 and ended in 1882. A strict set of emergency measures were implemented under the Anglo-French plan. The interest rate on the foreign loans was reduced to 5 per cent; the pay of the army, civil servants, and workmen employed by the government was cut; and a series of sales taxes (similar to VAT) were introduced on food and goods. The plan restored financial stability. But, in the process, it brought misery to the vast majority of the Egyptian people, and led to starvation in upper Egypt, increased unemployment, street rioting and, finally, a rebellion in the army.

In 1882 an Egyptian nationalist movement under the leadership of Arabi Pasha, a colonel in the Egyptian army, was on the verge of taking power. The nationalists wanted an end to Turkish dominance in government and Anglo-French control of the economy. By this stage law and order in Egypt had virtually collapsed. On 11 June a nationalist riot in Alexandria led to the death of 50 Europeans. This prompted the British government to order the formal occupation of Egypt. The Royal Navy bombarded, the British army invaded, and by October 1882 the rebellion had been crushed. Arabi Pasha was exiled to Ceylon, and Britain became 'the Government of Egypt'. Tewfik, Ismail's successor, was left in nominal charge but he was a mere figurehead. The British quickly ended Anglo-French 'dual control', much to the annoyance of the French, and stayed in Egypt until 1922.

The occupation effectively ended the long-held French hope of dominating an independent Egypt and led to bitter recriminations betweeen Britain and France which were to last for over 20 years. The cause of French outrage was not the occupation itself, which France had refused to join, but the British decision to rule the country on its own. This led to a French suspicion that Britain merely used the nationalist uprising as a cloak to hide its real desire to dominate Egypt and to freeze out France. The British attempt to allay French fears by ordering the withdrawal of Egyptian forces from the Sudan in 1884 ended in the siege at Kharthoum, the death of General Gordon, a British humiliation, and the withdrawal of British troops. In the late-1890s the British took revenge for Gordon's death by using armed force to annex the Sudan. This provoked more French anger and led to the 'Fashoda Incident' of 1898. This was a bungled attempt by a poorly equipped French expedition to capture the fort at Fashoda in western Sudan. The incident almost led to war between Britain and France, but the French government eventually backed down and agreed to the Sudan becoming a British 'sphere of influence'.

Advertisement for Pear's Soap (1887)

b) West Africa

The British government viewed West Africa with a great deal of detachment once the slave trade was outlawed in 1807. In 1865 a parliamentary select committee suggested that there should be no further colonial expansion in the region. The only reason Britain remained interested was due to the trade in palm oil which was used as an industrial lubricant and for the manufacture of soap - a thriving consumer growth industry in the late-nineteenth century. The leading British supplier of palm oil was George Goldie. He established a monopoly over the collection of palm oil on the River Niger through his United Africa Company (later renamed the Royal Niger Company). Goldie engaged in what the Foreign Office called 'creeping imperialism' by extending his economic interests inland from Accra. The British settlements of Sierra Leone and the Gold Coast were also expanded without government approval.

However, it was not Goldie or the British government who were the leading forces in the Partition of West Africa. France, Germany and King Leopold of the Belgians all played much more prominent roles. The French moved inland from Senegal and had ambitions to create a West African Empire. In 1882 the colonial agents of King Leopold arrived, signed treaties with several West African rulers, and set up the Congo Free State which developed a thriving rubber industry. Not surprisingly, the arrival of King Leopold alarmed the French who moved quickly inland from Gabon to create the French Congo. The British now became worried about the ambitions of the French and Leopold and signed a treaty with Portugal in February 1884 which recognised the ancient right of Portugal to the mouth of the Congo River. The whole situation grew even more complicated when Germany, led by Otto von Bismarck, seized Togoland and the Cameroons. The German Chancellor then shrewdly suggested that the European powers should settle their differences over territory peacefully by agreement. He suggested that this be done at a conference to be held in Berlin.

In December 1884 representatives of the major European powers met in Berlin in order to reach a settlement of the boundaries, trade and the rules of occupation in West Africa. The treaty they signed in 1885 agreed that there should be free trade in the Congo basin, recognised British economic interests on the Niger, and laid down ground rules for future annexation of territory in Africa. After the Berlin conference all a European power needed to do after grabbing land in Africa was to inform the other European powers that they were in 'effective occupation'. This arrangement speeded up the partition in the remainder of West Africa. The French took the majority of the available territory - which was mostly desert - and created French West Africa. The British gained a monopoly over the palm oil trade on the Niger River and created Nigeria. The Germans expanded in Togoland and the

Cameroons. King Leopold gained recognition for his Congo Free State as a territory under his personal (rather than his country's) control.

c) East Africa

The partition of East Africa involved three powers: Britain, Germany and Italy. The major British interest in the region was trade with the island of Zanzibar. The British government had no plans to take formal control of any part of East Africa prior to the Partition. The leading 'man on the spot' and driving force behind British expansion in the region was Sir William McKinnon, a Scot who had built his fortune in the shipping trade. He believed - quite irrationally - that East Africa had enormous economic potential. The Imperial British East Africa Company was set up by McKinnon to attract investment to the area. Karl Peters, a German explorer, had similar plans. In 1884 he founded the rival German East Africa Company, signed treaties with local rulers in Tanganyika, and gained official backing for his efforts from Bismarck, the German Chancellor.

This intervention of Germany prompted the British government to give similar support to McKinnon. As a result, East Africa was divided by diplomatic agreement into British and German 'spheres of influence' between 1885 and 1895. Germany took control of Tanganyika. The British expanded to control Uganda, Kenya, Zanzibar, Pemba, and British Somaliland. At first, the British government left the administration of East Africa to the British East Africa Company. This proved beyond it. By 1895 the British government was in formal control of a largely unwanted East African empire.

Italy was the third European power to grab territory in East Africa by capturing Eritrea in 1882 and a large part of Somaliland in 1889. In 1896 Italy attacked Abbysinia (now Ethiopia), the last truly independent African state, and was defeated. This was the only occasion during the Partition on which an African state successfully resisted a European aggressor.

d) Southern Africa

The Partition of southern Africa was really a tale of Anglo-Boer rivalry and the ambitions of Cecil Rhodes, a British multi-millionaire who was the most famous 'man on the spot' of all. He arrived in South Africa in 1870, aged 17, full of ambition, and quickly made a fortune from diamond mining. He developed a 'big idea' for the expansion of the British Empire, as the following extract reveals:

1 I contend that we are the first race of the world and that the more of
  the world we inhabit the better it is for the human race. I contend
  that every acre added to our territory means the birth of more of

the English race who otherwise would not be brought into
5 existence. Added to this, the absorption of the greater portion of
the world under our rule simply means the end to all wars ... The
furtherence of the British Empire, for bringing the whole of the
uncivilised world under British rule, for the recovery of the United
States, for making the Anglo-Saxon race but one Empire. What a
10 dream! but yet it is possible. It is possible!

Standing in the way of Rhodes' 'impossible dream' were the
independent Boer republics - the Transvaal and the Orange Free State.
The Boers were white, Protestant, Dutch in origin, fiercely independent, and generally scornful of 'Liberal England'. They had originally
settled on the southern tip of Africa but - as we saw earlier - they had
moved north during the 'great trek' of the late 1830s to create
independent states.

The Boers' insatiable desire for land created a great deal of
antagonism, not only with Britain, but also with a large number of
African tribal peoples. The most important were the Zulus, proud
people, skilled in war and diplomacy. This enabled them to create what
amounted to an anti-Boer coalition consisting of a large number of
South African tribal peoples. The Transvaal became so frightened of the
Zulu threat that they called on the British government - as what they saw
as the lesser of two evils - to protect them. All this did was place the Zulu
problem in the lap of the British government. In 1877 Britain took
control of the Transvaal. The British then quickly issued an ultimatum
to the Zulus, giving them two options. They could either disband their
large army or face war with the 'mighty' British Empire. The Zulus
chose war and were eventually defeated in 1879 after a valiant struggle.

The Zulu problem was no longer a factor in the way of British
expansion in southern Africa but it was also no longer a restraint on the
ambitions of the Boer republics. Shortly after the Zulu defeat the
Transvaal asked Britain to restore its independence. The British
refused. The Transvaal responded by attacking and defeating British
forces at Majuba Hill in 1881. Following this set-back Gladstone's
government agreed to restore control over domestic affairs to the
Transvaal. The Transvaal government took this to mean that their
country was fully independent. However, this was not Britain's
understanding of the situation, as the wording of the agreements signed
in 1882 and 1884 had left room for Britain to intervene in the domestic
affairs of the Transvaal at some future date.

The discovery of gold and diamonds in Cape Colony and in the
Boer republics was a 'mineral revolution' which transformed the
economic fortunes of Cape Colony and the Transvaal. The
Germans now began to take a greater interest in southern Africa for
the first time. In 1884 they declared a protectorate over South West
Africa (modern Namibia). The British responded by declaring a

protectorate over Bechuanaland (modern Botswana).

In the early 1890s Cecil Rhodes, by now Prime Minister of Cape Colony, swiftly and ruthlessly expanded British rule. He captured the area that became known as Northern and Southern Rhodesia (modern Zambia and Zimbabwe) and made Nyasaland (modern Malawi) a British protectorate. By 1895 he was ready to deal with the Boer republics once and for all. He encouraged British settlers to work in his diamond mines in the Transvaal and to agitate for voting rights. The Transvaal government correctly saw this as a deliberate plot to undermine the country's independence. In 1895 Rhodes supported an armed coup aimed at seizing control of the Transvaal. He left the planning to Dr Jameson, an old friend who fancied himself a military genius but was more of a Colonel Blimp. Jameson thought a raiding party of 500 armed men would be enough to overthrow the Transvaal government. This was a major blunder. A planned uprising of the Uitlanders (as the Boers called the British mine workers) never materialised. The Boers had little difficulty in rounding up Jameson's small force.

The incident (known as the Jameson Raid) was a deep humiliation for the British government. Joseph Chamberlain, the Colonial Secretary, and Lord Salisbury, the Prime Minister, were forced publicly to deny any knowledge of the raid (although it appears that Chamberlain was implicated). This left Cecil Rhodes to carry the can and he resigned. A broken man, he died in 1902.

In 1897, Sir Alfred Milner was appointed British High Commissioner for South Africa. Milner, a passionate imperialist, was supposedly appointed as a peacemaker in Southern Africa. But only days before his departure he was telling a friend that he was going to 'teach those bloody Boers a lesson'. Milner was to play a leading role in the events which led to the the Anglo-Boer War (often called the Boer War) of 1899-1902. This event is so important for understanding the development of the Empire between 1895 and 1914 it will discussed in greater depth in chapter 6. It was the last great act of British involvement in the Partition.

2 Interpretations

The Partition of Africa has produced a vast range of theories and interpretations and in a book of this size it would be impossible to do justice to them all. What can be done is to identify the three broad approaches into which they can be categorised. They can all be used to explain why each of the European powers became involved. A 'metropolitan' approach focuses on the motivations of each European power (metropole) and explains why each one joined in the Partition. 'Peripheral' approaches look at the problem from an African perspective and seek to show why each African region (periphery) was captured by a European power. An 'international relations' approach sets the Partition within a global framework. Each approach has been applied to explain the roles of Britain and the other European powers. However, no one approach has been generally accepted and the historical debate over the causes of the Partition remains a classic 'argument without end'.

a) Metropolitan Theories

i) J.A.Hobson: Overseas Investment

The best known metropolitan explanation was advanced in *Imperialism: A Study* (1902) by J.A. Hobson. This is a purely economic explanation, which views the Partition as a deliberately thought-out British policy designed by a shady élite of 'financiers, capital investors and unscrupulous politicians' who supported investment in new areas of the world rather than high wages and improved living conditions for the British worker. This led to a maldistribution of wealth. Hobson argued that while the rich had too much wealth and were encouraged to invest abroad, and the poor had so little in disposable income to spend, British industry could not expand. J.A. Hobson used economic statistics to support his interpretation. They do show a rapid increase in British overseas investment from £144 million in 1862 to £1,698 million in 1893. The Partition of Africa was, therefore, the British government supporting the aims of a small élite group of 'greedy capitalist' investors in Africa.

The impact Hobson made on the study of imperialism has been enormous. Yet his views have met with heavy criticism. D.K. Fieldhouse in *Economics and Empire* (1973) argues that Hobson failed to make a clear distinction about where British investment went in the late-nineteenth century. The largest proportion went to the settlement colonies, the USA, and Latin America - not tropical Africa. The importance Hobson assigned to the link between overseas investment and British involvement is debatable. In the case of Malaya investment only followed after annexation. The protection of the Suez canal and the route to India have also been shown to have been vitally important in determining British invervention in Egypt, East Africa and Southern Africa.

ii) Lenin: Crisis of Capitalism

Imperialism: The Highest Stage of Capitalism (1916) by V.I. Lenin was another purely economic explanation. Lenin was the leader of the Marxist-inspired Bolshevik Party and the leader of the 1917 Russian Revolution. He believed that 'a crisis in the capitalist economic system' in the late-nineteenth century was the main reason for European expansion in Africa. In his view, there were too many nations chasing too few markets. The free-trade era was abandoned by Britain's economic rivals in favour of protectionism, cut-throat competition, and colonial rivalry. According to Lenin, European governments during the Partition were simply acting in the interests of 'finance capitalists' and 'monopoly companies' in their attempts to dominate sources of raw materials in Africa. He saw the European governments who agreed to expansion as the 'puppets' of capitalist businessmen. For Lenin, the Partition was the beginning of a more advanced stage of capitalist development which involved financiers and industrial producers attempting to gain a monopoly control over the supplies of raw materials for industrial production. Lenin believed that the only cure for imperialism was a revolution by the people. This would destroy capitalism and put an end to imperialism.

iii) Schumpeter: Crisis of Hereditary Élites

The Sociology of Imperialism (1951) by J.A. Schumpeter is a very important non-economic explanation. He defined imperialism as 'the objectless disposition on the part of a state to unlimited forcible expansion' and attacked the view that imperialism was linked to modern capitalism. Instead Schumpeter argued that the group who supported imperialism were old aristocractic hereditary élites who passed on ideas of imperial glory and aristocratic breeding and superiority from generation to generation.

It was 'old hereditary aristocratic élites', rather than capitalist businessmen or financiers, who Schumpeter believed were the leading forces behind the Partition of Africa. He thought that the aristocratic forces of Europe were seeking power and imperial glory abroad because they felt in danger of extinction from the rising business classes and rising working-class movements. Schumpeter predicted that the end of imperialism would only come when the power of the aristocracy was weakened and when governments followed a purely capitalist policy of free trade.

Schumpeter's theory which was essentially designed to attack the link of earlier theories between finance capitalism and imperialism has also aroused criticism. To begin with, the British aristocracy never fitted this concept; a great many of them were 'progressive' 'gentlemanly capitalists' who favoured peaceful economic expansion and social reform. Most British imperial administrators of the new tropical colonies of Africa were not drawn from the heriditary peerage but from the professional middle class. King Leopold, who should be typical of those Schumpeter had in mind, was actually interested in Africa as a suitable candidate for scientific exploration, technological advance and economic reward. The idea that the decline of the aristocracy would lead to the end of wars for military conquest simply does not fit in with the history of military conflict in the twentieth century.

iv) Eric Hobsbawm: Industry and Empire

Eric Hobsbawm, in *Industry and Empire* (1968), highlighted the importance of technological changes in Europe in the late-nineteenth century brought about by the industrial revolution. He described the Gatling Gun, the machine gun, the telegraph, the railway, and the steamship as the 'tools of Empire'. He believed that the technological advantage industry gave Europeans made the conquest of weak pre-industrial people easier and encouraged a new wave of imperialism. According to Hobsbawm, the Partition of Africa would not have occurred without the advances in technology that the industrial revolution produced.

v) Peter Cain and Tony Hopkins: 'Gentlemanly Capitalism'

The greatest challenge to Marxist interpretations - especially Lenin's view that the 'New Imperialism' was linked to the industrial process - is that put forward by P.J. Cain and A.G. Hopkins in *British Imperialism: Innovation and Expansion 1688-1914* (1993). They reject the link between industrialisation and imperial expansion and instead argue that a great deal of continuity existed in the development of British imperial expansion from 1688 to 1914. The commercial, professional and landed élites of London and the south-east, who had led imperial expansion in the eighteenth century helped to create a financial and service based economy focused on the City of London. This sector of the British economy expanded rapidly in the nineteenth century. As new 'gentlemen' emerged and thrived during this financial revolution in the City of London they joined forces with existing London élites to form a new 'Gentlemanly Capitalist' élite. The values of this dominant group were those taught at the more prestigious public schools such as Eton, Harrow, Rugby and Winchester and at Oxford and Cambridge Universities. They combined the life of the metropolis with a country estate, intermarried with the old artistocracy, and created 'old-boy networks' which dominated the leading echelons of power and influence within the British government and the Empire. Cain and Hopkins suggest that the British government, almost by instinct, rather than by any conspiratorial collaboration, put the needs of these 'gentlemanly capitalists' above those of 'socially and culturally inferior' northern industrialists who had come to prominence during the 'Industrial Revolution'. After 1870 the 'gentlemanly capitalists' invested heavily abroad and exerted pressure on the British government to defend their interests whenever they were threatened by European rivals and nationalist movements. Although the government claimed it was defending 'National Interests' during the Partition of Africa, those interests, argue Cain and Hopkins, had really become the interests of 'Gentlemanly Capitalism' in London and the south-east.

This is a bold, provocative and thought provoking interpretation.

They claim that every other theory of British imperial expansion - especially the Marxist emphasis on industry - is inadequate. By assigning primacy to financial and service sectors of the British economy in explaining British imperial expansion, they claim to have created a 'new framework for interpreting Britain's historic role as a world power'. The interpretation firmly puts 'economic impulses emanating from the metropole' back at the centre of discussion. It rejects the fashion of concentrating on changes at the periphery which had been so influential over imperial historians since the revisionist arguments of Gallagher and Robinson burst on to the scene in the 1950s, and spawned a wake of new studies in the 1960s and 1970s.

The work of Cain and Hopkins is something of a partial rehabilitation of the views of J.A. Hobson, in particular, his contention that overseas expansion in the late nineteenth century was driven by the needs of 'finance capitalists'. But Cain and Hopkins reject Hobson's idea of a well thought out conspiracy between government and the City of London. Instead they offer up the idea that the government's conception of 'National Interests' coincided - wittingly and unwittingly - with the interests of 'gentlemanly capitalist' financiers during the age of the so called 'New Imperialism'. The decision makers on colonial matters were basically the same sort of people who belonged to the same exclusive élite. The interpretation has the added attraction of providing a long-term explanation for the City of London's survival, the dominance of the south-east in the current British economy and the decline of northern industry and the Empire in the twentieth century.

It may be that once the dust of academic battle has settled the 'gentlemanly capitalist' will prove to be yet another example of bending the facts to fit a theory. Trying to isolate exactly how the 'gentlemanly capitalists' of the nineteenth century influenced government policy and explaining how the government wittingly and unwittingly supported their aims may prove an impossible task. A number of prominent historians have already raised doubts about the Cain and Hopkins interpretation. Andrew Porter, a leading imperial historian, recently claimed in the *Journal of Imperial and Commonwealth History* (1990) that their theory of 'gentlemanly capitalism' is too Anglo-centric in that it implies the development of British imperialism can be exclusively explained by reference to British governing élites and financial élites in the metropole while ignoring wider European and international issues. Martin Daunton in an article in the history journal *Past and Present* (1989) suggested that the term 'gentlemanly capitalism' does not adequately explain the nature of the British economy in the late-nineteenth century. He claimed that the role played by industrialists is not readily distinguishable from the activities of financial interests in the City of London.

Only time - and more research - will tell who is right. It may be that the city and industry were not as divorced from each other as Cain and

Hopkins imagine. The complexity of the government-business relationship may prove to have been oversimplified. Yet whatever the outcome of the debate over their theory, Cain and Hopkins' work is likely to retain a crucial importance within imperial history because it has focused attention on the nature of ruling élites in the City of London and on their relationship to imperial expansion in the late-nineteenth century. It may be that the strength of the link has been exaggerated but it already appears that previous studies did not take enough account of its real significance in the rise and fall of the British Empire. The work of Cain and Hopkins - now deeply influential - has boldly suggested that the empire was no simple 'handmaiden of industrial capitalism' but was rather the work of 'gentlemen' who managed 'men not machines' in London and the south-east. They have claimed that the British 'industrial revolution' was a phenomenon which had little impact on the course of British imperialism. True or false, this is an argument which no historian can possibly ignore.

b) Peripheral Theories

All the above are metropolitan theories and focus exclusively on European motivations. They look at the Partition from the perspective of European states and societies. They tell us very little about the role of Africa and its people, who are seemingly acted upon rather than being active in the process. Peripheral explanations suggest that the Partition cannot by explained solely by reference to European society. A peripheral theory is, therefore, one that gives due account to explaining how changes within the regions of Africa interacted with European desires for expansion. This means that such theories integrate the African dimension into the European framework.

i) Gallagher and Robinson

Gallagher and Robinson have been the pioneers of this approach. In their book *Africa and the Victorians: The Official Mind of Imperialism* (1961) they argued that British involvement in the Partition of Africa was not motivated by a 'new' desire by government to support British investment. Instead they suggested that 'the official mind' of British imperialism in Whitehall followed a consistent policy towards the Empire throughout the nineteenth century in seeking 'informal' control of trade wherever possible and only supporting formal rule when trade was threatened by civil disorder or the ambitions of a rival power.

According to Gallagher and Robinson the engine room of British intervention was not problems in Europe but was a purely 'local crisis' in Egypt. This dragged a reluctant British government into the problems of north Africa and led to Anglo-French rivalry which proved a vital contributor to the partition of west Africa and created tension in the

Sudan. Likewise they view British expansion in Southern Africa to be primarily due to worries over the rise of the Transvaal and Boer nationalism. They claim that throughout the duration of the Partition the British looked at their strategic role in the world and took little notice of business lobbies or public opinion before deciding to intervene. The crucially important part of Gallagher and Robinson's work is the importance they give to 'pull factors' in Africa which influenced Britain to become involved.

ii) The 'Men on the Spot' Factor

This interpretation, which has been advanced by a number of historians, emphasises the role played by 'men on the spot' in Africa who encouraged their governments to become involved. Rhodes in South Africa, Peters and McKinnon in East Africa, Goldie in West Africa and the role of French and Belgian colonial agents have all come under scrutiny. It has been claimed that these men had grand schemes of their own, that they worked with the local power brokers to get them under way, and that they then gained the support of their governments to complete the process.

iii) African Nationalism

African historians have undertaken important research into the role played by Africans during the Partition. They have shown how African nationalism was crucial in Egypt, the Sudan, Abyssinia and in southern Africa; how African rulers, states and merchants collaborated with European powers; and how other African tribes such as the Zulus (in South Africa), the Ashanti (in the Gold Coast) and the Mashona (in Southern Rhodesia) fought bravely to retain their independence. It has also been shown how African leaders sought agreements with different European powers. A good example of how this tribal diplomacy worked can be be found in a letter from King Bell and King Acqua to Gladstone.

1 Dear Mr. Gladstone,
   We both your servants have met this afternoon to write you these few lines of writing trusting it may find you in a good state of health as it leaves us at present. As we heard you are the chief man in the
5 House of Commons, so we may write to tell you that we want to be under Her Majesty's control. We want our country to be governed by the British government. We are tired of governing this country ourselves, every dispute leads to war, and often great loss of lives, so we think it is best thing to give up the country to you British men
10 with no doubt will bring peace, civilisation and Christianity in the country. Do for mercy's sake please lay our request before the queen and to the rulers of the British Government. Do, sir, for

Government. Do, sir, for mercy sake, please assist us in this
important undertaking. We heard that you are a good man, so we
15 hope that you will do all you can in you power to see that our
request is granted. We are quite willing to abolish all heathen
customs. No doubt god will bless you for putting a light in our
country. Please to send us an answer as quick as you can.

King Bell and King Acqua
of the Cameroons River, West Africa
6 November 1881

In general the pleas of African leaders fell on deaf ears. For example,
Gladstone did not even reply to this request, and at the Berlin
Conference the British agreed to the German conquest of the
Cameroons.

Clearly, peripheral explanations do provide a balance to metropolitan
approaches which claim the partition can only be explained by the
actions of European capitalists, financiers, governments, industry and
aristocrats. As a reaction against these approaches peripheral theory
shows that social, economic and political factors in Africa played a much
greater role within the process than has often been recognised. Most
metropolitan theories assume that all the decisions relating to
imperialism were made by a very few Europeans located in the major
capitalist nations. It is therefore only to be expected that many older
accounts of imperial history view the Partition in terms of what
Europeans did, how they did it, and why they did it - in fact, as a mere
'sideshow' to events in Europe. This does no justice to the importance of
Africans in the process.

c) International Relations Theories

Another development in the study of imperialism has been the use of
international relations theories to explain the Partition. These
approaches set the Partition of Africa within a global framework.

i) A.J.P. Taylor: The Primacy of Political and Diplomatic Factors

A.J.P. Taylor in *The Struggle for Mastery in Europe* (1954) gave primacy
to the political and diplomatic aims of the leading European powers.
Taylor believed that the Partition was due to changes in European
power politics and society. He suggested that the victory of Germany in
the Franco-Prussian War of 1871 unhinged the balance of power in
Europe, created a deadlock in European politics, and encouraged the
growth of militant nationalism, which found expression in overseas
expansion.

Taylor described Europe after 1870 as 'an armed camp' with the
balance of power being so delicately poised that any small conflict within

the continent was likely to produce war. He maintained that in these circumstances the partition of Africa provided a safe arena for European competition for expansion without the risk of producing a European war. His view was that the Partition constituted a totally unplanned and irrational extension to Africa of 'the struggle for mastery in Europe'.

D.K. Fieldhouse and a number of other diplomatic historians once favoured this argument. But in his later work, such as *Economics and Empire* (1973), Fieldhouse placed far greater emphasis on economic problems in Africa which he believed pulled the European powers into the region.

ii) Paul Kennedy: The Rise and Fall of Great Powers

A broader international relations approach which looks beyond Europe is put forward by Paul Kennedy in *The Rise and Fall of the Great Powers* (1988). The book examines the Partition within the context (or grand sweep) of the rise and fall of the major powers of world history. Kennedy suggests that the industrial revolution made Britain the most dominant power in the world between 1815 and 1870. During this period Britain created a new model of great power status, based on free trade, industry, naval power, investment, and colonies. In Kennedy's view, the Partition of Africa happened because other European powers sought to emulate the British path to great power status. As European powers expanded in Africa, the British responded and seized colonies. He therefore concludes that British involvement was driven by a desire to defend her dominance of international trade and imperial rule.

This argument is attractive as it looks at the issue within a global framework and combines evidence from metropolitan and peripheral approaches. It also has the advantage of explaining the motivations of all the European powers. It seems likely that the 'international relations' approach will feature strongly in the future debate over the causes of the Partition of Africa.

3 Britain, the European Powers and the Partition: An Assessment

It is clear that the mountain of interpretations which have been put forward to explain the Partition of Africa has produced no consensus on why Britain and the other European powers became involved. It seems that the reasons for the participation are complex and do not lend themselves to a simple explanation. However, it does seem worthwhile attempting a brief survey of the probable motives of each of the European powers which joined in the Partition.

a) Britain

The argument that Britain's reasons for becoming involved in the Partition of Africa were a mixture of power politics and economic necessity appears impossible to deny. This view fits most British actions during the Partition. For example, it particularly seems to make sense of the events that led up to the occupation of Egypt. It was a fear that the Suez Canal might fall into the hands of a rival power which lay behind much of what was done. Of course, all historians would agree with the assessment thus far. The issue that remains unresolved, and a matter of major controversy, is the balance between political and economic motives. Perhaps the judgement whether Britain acted more from a desire to protect and/or increase her power than from a wish to protect and/or add to her wealth will always have to be made depending on the observer's values and prejudices. Certainly there is plenty of evidence to support both points of view.

Any argument which sees the British government as a 'reluctant' participant in the Partition is persuasive. The slow and deliberate way in which the British government reacted both to events in Africa and to the activities of rival European powers during the early stages of the Partition certainly adds weight to this interpretation. However, it must be remembered that there was never any doubt that the vast growth of British investment in north and southern Africa was going to be protected, and therefore too much should not be read into the reluctance. The Victorian 'frame of mind' was never passionate, always appeared reluctant, but in practice never flinched from defending British economic interests whenever and wherever they were felt to be threatened.

b) Germany

In the case of Germany we see a greater interest in purely political objectives. Germany was determined to become the dominant European power and colonial issues were very much used to further this end. In particular, up to 1890 while Otto von Bismarck was Chancellor, German aims were clearly centred on Europe. The case for arguing that Bismarck used colonial problems for political ends is persuasive. He said that, 'My map of Africa is in Europe. Here lies Russia and here lies France, that is my map of Africa'. In January 1889 he said in a Reichstag speech that he viewed colonial expansion with 'the gravest apprehension' and insisted that in Africa Germany should proceed 'slowly and in agreement with England'. Bismarck also used colonial victories for the political objective of winning elections. He won the 1884 German election on the wave of euphoria produced by his colonial triumph in West Africa.

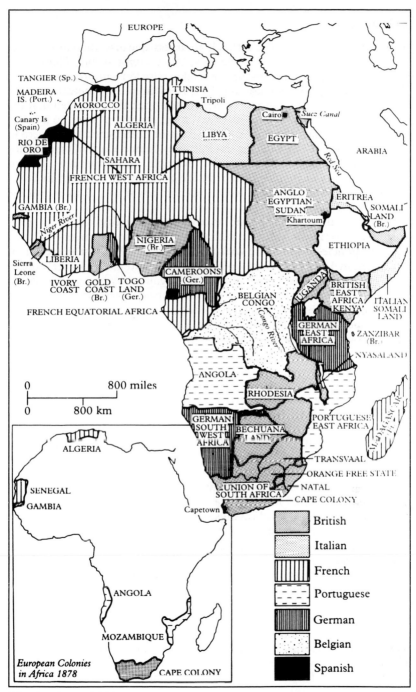

The Partition of Africa 1878 and 1914

c) France

France's motives are more difficult to assess because the country was divided over what the policy towards Africa ought to be. There were pro-imperialists who advocated colonial expansion - in order to restore the national pride which had been dented by defeat in the Franco-Prussian War - and there were anti-imperialists who felt that the Partition was an unwelcome diversion from the more pressing need to take revenge against Germany. Politicians of both persuasions were in power at different times during the Partition, hence a lack of consistency in the policies that were followed. For example, anti-imperialists missed the opportunity of joining Britain in the occupation of Egypt in 1882, while pro-imperialists almost led France into a war with Britain over the Sudan in 1898.

However, the French public as a whole never displayed any great enthusiasm for imperialism. In fact, when French governments followed imperial policies not in tune with public opinion they lost power. This happened in 1881 over Tunis in North Africa and in 1885 over Tonkin in Indo-China. There were few votes to be gained by being jingoistic in France. It is true that the French did see economic benefits to be gained in North Africa, but there is no evidence of a 'capitalist plot'. The view that France became involved in the Partition for reasons of dented national pride remains the most attractive.

d) The Minor European Powers

Of the remaining European participants in the Partition, the activities of Belgium and King Leopold have attracted the most attention. King Leopold emerges as the only European statesmen with a clear plan to acquire territory in Africa. Yet he had little backing from the Belgian government for his expansionist policy, and he was forced to play a remarkably personal role.

Leopold had dreamed of a Belgian colonial empire since the 1860s. He became interested in acquiring territory after hearing the reports of the British explorers David Livingstone and Verney Lovett Cameron. In 1876 he invited a distinguished group of geographers and explorers to Brussels to discuss the potential of Africa and out of this came the International Africa Association, which claimed to bring the benefits of 'science and civilisation' to Africa. Lord Rosebery, the Foreign Secretary, said he would be more able to accept Leopold's sincerity 'if he looked a little less like Fagin' (a villainous character in Dickens' novel, *Oliver Twist*). King Leopold actually behaved like Fagin. He ran the Congo purely for economic gain and his agents treated the Africans who worked in the Congo rubber industry with merciless barbarity. This cruel exploitation was the biggest scandal of the Partition of Africa and was roundly condemned by the Belgian parliament.

It seems clear that Italy was largely motivated by a desire for enhanced international status. Italians also felt there were possible economic benefits in Africa. There were some successes but, of course, the Italian bid for colonies ended in a national humiliation when they were defeated by the Abyssinians at the battle of Adowa in 1896.

The roles of Portugal and Spain were relatively insignificant as both nations simply attempted to preserve their existing interests. Therefore the part they played in the Partition was almost completely defensive, and seems to have been driven by a desire to retain some symbol of the countries' glorious pasts.

Making Notes on 'The Partition of Africa'

This chapter covers an extremly popular examination topic in both British and European courses. You would therefore be well advised to make fairly detailed notes.

You need to have three aims at the start of your note-making:
i) To gain a clear grasp of the key events of the Partition,
ii) To build up an understanding of the various interpretations, and
iii) To acquire an appreciation of why each of the European powers played the part it did in the Partition.

You may find that the following headings and questions will provide a suitable structure for your note-making.

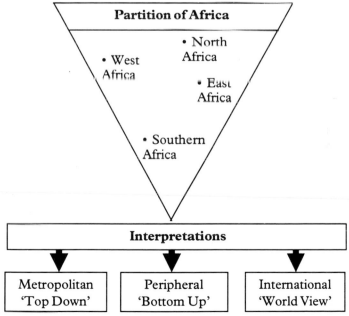

Summary - The Partition of Africa

1   North Africa. The occupation of Egypt is clearly vital. What role was played by economic factors? What impact did the occupation have on Anglo-French relations?
2   West Africa. What was the major issue? What were the ambitions of Germany and of King Leopold? What was the significance of the Berlin Conference?
3   East Africa. How important were the roles of McKinnon and Peters?
4   South Africa. How important was Anglo-Boer rivalry? Why was the role of Cecil Rhodes important?
5   Interpretations. In your own words explain what is meant by a 'metropolitan', a 'peripheral', and an 'international relations' theory. Give an example of each. Note down the distinguishing features of each of the leading metropolitan and peripheral theories and summarise the arguments that have been put forward in criticism of each of them. For example, on what basis have Gallagher and Robinson attacked the views of Hobson and Lenin?
6   Britain and the European Powers. Summarise the explanation given of each country's motives. Remembering that the views expressed are opinion rather than fact, be prepared to note down where you disagree with them and why.

Answering essay questions on 'The Partition of Africa'

A wide range of questions can be set on the Partition of Africa. A typical example of a question on the role of Britain in the Partition is,

1   To what extent were British actions during the Partition of Africa 'reluctant'?

This is a teasing question. It tempts you to assume that 'British actions' is a coherent concept. However, if you fall into the trap that the examiner has set you will almost certainly end up in a muddle. This is a good example of the need to study the wording of questions very carefully, because in this case if you do not pick up the fact that you must distinguish between the component parts of 'British actions' you will be in danger of going round and round in circles. Make your decision about how you will separate out the different aspects of 'British actions'. Will you treat the government as a single aspect or will you make a distinction between, say, Gladstone and Chamberlain? Equally, will the 'men on the spot' be lumped together, or would you wish to separate Rhodes from Goldie or McKinnon? Once you have 'unpacked' 'British actions' by making a list of the people or groups you intend to discuss separately the question should become very manageable. There should be no difficulty in finding several things to say about reluctance or lack of it in each case.

In papers on European history questions on the Partition normally ask that the role of all the European powers - including Britain - is considered. Study the following examples:-

2   To what extent was the Partition of Africa in the late-nineteenth century a product of economic factors?
3   Assess the motives of the various European powers in the Partition of Africa.

Question 2 needs to be approached in the same way that all 'to what extent/how far?' questions are best tackled. First of all, the explanation suggested in the question (in this case 'economic factors') needs to be unpacked by identifying its component parts. Here there are three. What are they? Then the other possible explanations need to be identified. These all have to do with politics, and can probably best be divided into those arising from internal politics (particularly think about Bismarck in this context) and those that relate to international relations. By carrying out these two analytical tasks you should have identified five separate points, each of which will require at least one example to illustrate it. Decide which examples you will use. Now you must make up your mind about the relative importance of the economic (3 aspects) and the political (2 aspects) factors so that you can comment on the 'to what extent?' aspect of the question directly. Whatever you decide it will probably be sensible to deal with the economic factors first as this is the focus of the question.

The key word in question 3 is 'assess'. To tackle this question successfully requires a very clear idea of what this instruction implies. How does 'assess' differ from 'describe' or 'explain'? You might come to the conclusion that in order to assess you must describe and explain, but that you must do other things as well. Effective assessment can only be carried out according to criteria that have been consciously identified. It is always best to use the introduction in an 'assessment' essay to state the criteria you are going to use. What are appropriate criteria to use when assessing motives? Once you have decided this the shape of your answer to question 3 will be becoming clear.

It is possible that some examiners may set a question on the debate over the Partition of Africa. A typical example is:

4   Comment on the strengths and weaknesses of the main interpretations that have been put forward to explain the Partition of Africa.

This is another example of a straightforward question where success will depend upon a clear understanding of the key instruction. This time it is 'comment on'. What are the implications of this phrase? Clearly there is an element of 'describe' in it. But there is much more than that. If you tackle such a question without having first made decisions about what this 'much more' is, you will be throwing away about half the available marks before you begin. So thinking carefully about key instructions is undoubtedly a vital part of essay planning.

Source-based questions on 'The Partition of Africa'

1 Stephen Cave on Egypt's Financial Crisis
Carefully read the extracts on page 29. Answer the following questions.
a) Who does Cave blame for Egypt's economic problems? (4 marks)
b) Why should the evidence of Cave be treated with caution? (5 marks)
c) Comment on the accuracy of Cave's assessment in the light of your other knowledge about the Egyptian financial crisis. (6 marks)

2 Cecil Rhodes' view of British Imperialism
Carefully read the extract on pages 33-4. Answer the following questions.
a) What does Rhodes mean by the phrase 'I contend that we are the first race of the world'? (2 marks)
b) Summarise the other main points that Rhodes is putting forward in the extract. (4 marks)
c) What do Rhodes' views suggest about the way he might act as the leader of Cape Colony? (4 marks)
d) Comment on the practicality of the aspirations Rhodes expressed. (5 marks)

3 An African plea to Gladstone
Carefully read the extract on pages 41-2.
Answer the following questions.
a) Summarise the contents of the letter. (3 marks)
b) What are the strengths and weaknesess of the letter as a historical source? (7 marks)

4 Advertisement on 'The Formula for British Conquest'
Carefully study the advertisement for Pears soap on on page 31. Answer the following questions.
a) What conclusions can be drawn from the way in which the Africans in the advertisement are depicted? (3 marks)
b) How does Robinson portray the Africans in the comments at the bottom of the advertisement. Do you believe his report? Explain your answer. (5 marks)
c) What does the advertisement tell us about the way in which the Partition was portrayed to a British audience? (5 marks)

CHAPTER 4

The British Empire in Asia, 1815-1914

No study of the British Empire in the period 1815-1914 would be complete without a full examination of Asia, the third largest market for British goods and home to the vast sub-continent of India - the 'Jewel in the Crown' of the British Empire in the Victorian age. The largest single element of British army spending was devoted to the Indian army. The first task of the Royal Navy was to protect the trade route to India. The anti-Russian tone of British foreign policy, the purchase of shares in the Suez Canal, and the 'open door' policy with China were all linked in one way or another to India. The mere thought that India was threatened by rebellion or attack sent shock waves through the ruling élites of British society. British policy with the rest of Asia was always formulated with India very much in mind.

Three important aspects of British imperial activity in Asia during this period will be given close scrutiny in this chapter: the development of British rule in India (a classic case of 'formal' rule); the 'open door' policy with China (a classic case of 'informal' imperialism); and the spread of 'New Imperialism' to Asia, which almost ended with a Partition of China, and which contributed to the abandonment of 'splendid isolation' by Britain.

1 The Development of British Rule in India

a) Background

Lord Curzon, the most famous Viceroy of India, once claimed that 'as long as we rule India, we are the greatest power in the world. If we lose it, we shall drop straightaway to a third rate power'. It is easy to understand why he thought this way. India covered a staggering 1,766,597 square miles of land (larger than all of Europe, excluding Russia) with a population of 294 million people in 1901. At its height the British 'Raj' covered 61.5 per cent of Indian territory. In 1900 it was divided into seven provinces: Bombay, Bengal, Madras, the Punjab, the Central Provinces, the North-western provinces, and the North West frontier provinces. The remaining 38.5 per cent of territory consisted of 601 disparate 'princely states'. Technically, the 'princely states' were not part of 'British India'. Yet they were not independent either. Nearly all of them owed allegiance to the British Crown. Treaties signed by the princes with Britain left domestic policy in their control and protected them from external attack and internal rebellion, but left control of their foreign and defence policies in the hands of the Crown. No Indian prince was allowed to travel abroad without the express permission of the Viceroy. In 1901 a total of 62,461,549 people lived in 'the princely states' while 231,899,507 people were under formal British rule in the seven provinces of 'British India'.

The story of how Britain came to rule this enormous and magnificent sub-continent falls into two distinct phases. The first runs from the seventeenth century to the Indian Mutiny of 1857-8. This period was dominated by the establishment and expansion of British rule under the privately owned East India Company (albeit under increasing direction of the British government from 1784 onwards). The second phase - the period of 'the British Raj' - runs from 1858 to 1947, when India was granted independence. This period was characterised by formal British rule and the rise of Indian nationalism. The turning point between the two phases was the Indian Mutiny.

b) The East India Company

The rise to dominance of the British in India began in the seventeenth century when traders from the East India Company were granted a Royal Charter in 1600 by Queen Elizabeth I. On arrival in India the Company quickly established a series of trading areas - Surat (1612), Madras (1640), Bombay (1661) and Calcutta (1690) - and recruited local Indian soldiers (sepoys) to defend their economic interests. Among the first items exported to India from Britain were woollen vests, wrought iron, and 'hard wearing Devon trousers'.

British rule expanded at the expense of the Muslim Mughal Emperor - a direct descendent of Genghis Khan, whose Mongolian cavalry army had conquered Northern India in the thirteenth century. The Mughal Emperors ruled through a series of alliances with regional Hindu and Muslim rulers (described by British historians as 'princes'). The system was never very stable as many Indian princes were extremely powerful, and essentially acted as if they were independent. The last effective Mughal Emperor was Aurangzeb, who died in 1707. After his death the Mughal Empire gradually split apart. The local princes became, more or less, independent rulers of their own provinces.

The real drive to extend the British interests in India began with the annexation of Bengal - the largest Indian province - following the battle of Plassey in 1757. This occurred shortly after the East India Company had appointed Robert Clive, who became known later as 'Clive of India', to extend the territory under its control. He brought Calcutta and Bengal - the largest part of the Mughal Empire - under the control of the company, negotiated important trade agreements with the numerous independent regional princes, pushed the French out of India, and persuaded the Mughal Emperor to grant monopoly trading rights to the East India Company. By the late-eighteenth century the East India Company not only had a monopoly over European trade with India but had also emerged as a major political power in India with responsibilities for law, order, administration, trade, defence and diplomacy. By this time the Company - run by London merchants - resembled a state more than a private company.

By the late-eighteenth century this state of affairs provoked criticism. Demands were made in parliament for greater regulation and supervision of the Company. The British government also began to doubt whether it was correct for a trading company to have such enormous responsibilities for such a large part of the Empire. At the same time, the Company began to find the costs of administering and defending the territories extremely high. The costs of defence and administration escalated, debts mounted, the value of shares in the Company slumped, and profits collapsed. In 1773 the Company which had been portrayed by its critics as 'a corrupt monopoly' called on the British government for help to rule the areas under its control.

The British government responded by taking several measures between 1773 and 1833 which served to place the East India Company in a subservient role. Indeed it would be fair to say that from 1773 to 1858 the British government ruled India through the agency of the East India Company. The India Act (1774) gave the British government 'the power of guiding the politics of India with as little means of corrupt influence as possible'. The Company retained ownership rights over its captured territory, a trade monopoly and existing responsibilities over civil administration and defence. A British Governor-General, appointed by a council of four, nominated by the Cabinet and the Company was given overall political, legal and diplomatic control over British territory in India. In 1784 an Indian Board of Control was set up to supervise Indian affairs. In 1813 the British government ended the Company's monopoly over Indian trade - except the trade in tea with China. In 1833 even this monopoly was ended.

All these measures served to turn the the East India Company into a 'bureaucratic shell' of its former self. It used to be argued that the British government broke the monopoly of the East India Company from 1773 onwards because the Company was corrupt, inefficient and unprofitable. This view has recently been called into question by Cain and Hopkins in *British Imperialism* (1993). They have shown that the East India Company was no 'creaking mercantilist monopoly', but a vibrant capitalist enterprise which generated wealth, and created the framework for British trade expansion throughout Asia. Philip Lawson in his recent study *The East India Company* (1993) has suggested that the British government took greater control over the Company because it came under pressure from British business interests which saw the Indian market as a vital area for their own expansion.

c) Expansion

After 1815 successive Governor-Generals expanded British rule in

India. Some historians have suggested that this was simply the result of unprovoked aggression. But this is incorrect. The causes were far more complex. The Mughal Empire was clearly in a state of decay and there was a resulting power vacuum. Many powerful local princes were asserting their independence. This created instability in some areas. As the British sought to defend their interests they frequently met with armed resistance. This often led to punitive expeditions and annexations. For example, the Pindaris of central India were attacked and were finally defeated at the Battle of Kirkee in 1824. By 1830 the British had dramatically extended the territory under their control or influence. By 1856 Sind, Punjab, Berar and Oudh had all been added.

This rapid expansion of British rule was accompanied by economic, social, and political changes. Lord William Bentinck, the Governor-General from 1828 to 1835, introduced a comprehensive policy of 'westernisation'. This controversial plan involved developing India along British lines. English was made the official language of law, administration and education. Several traditional Indian religious customs such as Sutee, (the Hindu practice of throwing widows onto the flaming funeral pyres of their dead husbands), and the human sacrifices and rituals of several secret societies were outlawed. Criminal bands known as Thugee (the origin of the English word 'thug') were suppressed.

The policy of westernisation disregarded cherished Indian religious, social and regional customs in a way that had never occurred before, even under Mughal rule. The result was growing resentment among the Indian people towards British rule. This found expression in the bloody and bitter Indian Mutiny of 1857.

2 The Indian Mutiny

a) Background

The immediate cause of the Mutiny is not disputed. Sepoys in the Indian army mutinied in 1857 after refusing to bite cartridges before loading them into the newly introduced Enfield rifle because they were said to contain cow and pig grease. They had refused on religious grounds as the cow is sacred to Hindus and the pig is considered to be unclean by Muslims. Yet the longer-term causes of the Indian Mutiny went much deeper than an argument about the loading of the Enfield rifle.

There were underlying economic grievances. After the monopoly of the East India Company had been ended in 1813, the sub-continent was opened up to the unfettered competition of British industrialists and merchants. India was progressively swamped by cheap British goods. British property developers bought up land, introduced a landlord system, and imposed high rents. Indian producers of export goods such

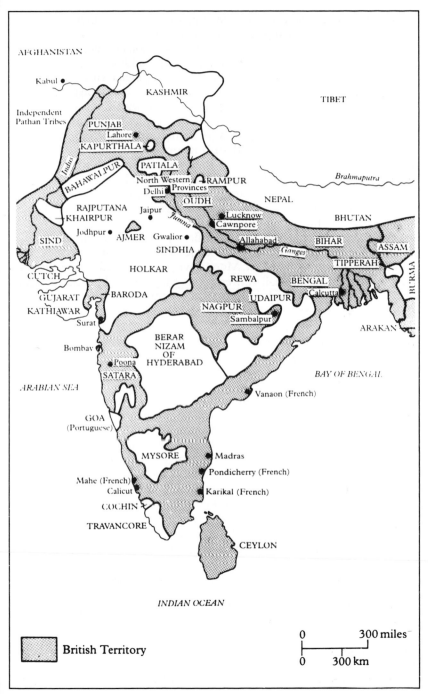

India on the eve of the Mutiny

as tea, indigo, and spices received very low prices for their products. There were also political grievances. Territorial expansion was greatly resented, especially the latest 'rash' of annexations - Punjab and Sind (1843), Berar (1853) and Oudh (1856). In addition, the policy of westernisation caused concern because it impinged so obviously on everyday life. Hundreds of village schools, a central legal council, national laws, a university, and a postal service with English style post offices were all established, and roads and canals were built. A large number of Indians felt that they were being forced to accept an 'alien' culture. But not only did the British ignore Indian feelings, they also failed to recognise the weakness of their own situation. British security depended on Indian sepoys recruited from the local Indian community. In 1857, out of a British Indian Army numbering 270,000 men, only 40,000 were of European origin. In some regions, 90 per cent of all men in the army were Indian.

Thus, the row over the Enfield rifle tapped a nerve in the sepoys which was connected to broader concerns about British rule. The Mutiny began after soldiers at Meerut who had refused to use the rifle were sentenced to long jail sentences in May 1857. The entire sepoy army in Meerut mutinied, killing all the British officers. The Mutiny quickly spread to Delhi, Oudh, Cawnpore and Lucknow. However, the majority of the Indian princes remained loyal, as did the sepoy units in Bengal, the Punjab, Bombay and Madras.

b) The Events of the Mutiny

The Mutiny was an extremely brutal affair which lasted just over a year. It took three months for British troops to restore order at Delhi where 40,000 sepoys had revolted. The struggle for Lucknow, the capital of Oudh, lasted 12 months before the British finally regained control against 60,000 mutineers. A very bitter struggle took place at Cawnpore. A small group of fewer than 1000 British men, women and children were starved into submission. General Neil, a British army commander, issued the following order to the officers leading the relief force:

> 1 The villages of Mugboon and neighbourhood to be attacked and destroyed; slaughter all the men; take no prisoners ... All sepoys found without papers from regiments that have mutinied who cannot give good accounts of themselves to be hanged forthwith.
> 5 Futtehpore to be promptly attacked, the Pathan quarters to be destroyed, all in it killed; in fact make a single example of this place.

On the day the British arrived the sepoys refused to surrender. Instead they threw the dead women over the city walls. The British soon crushed the revolt. A British officer described what he saw on his arrival in Cawnpore:

1 Ladies and children's bloody torn dresses and shoes were lying
about and locks of hair torn from their heads. The floor of the one
room they were all dragged into and killed was saturated with
blood ... I wish to show the natives of India that the punishment
5 inflicted by us for such deeds will be the heaviest, the most
revolting to their feelings, and what they must ever remember.

The British were true to their word. The captured sepoys were forced to
lick up the blood of their victims before being hanged one by one. The
bitter fighting went on for another year before the rebels were finally
defeated in June 1858. The reprisals inflicted by the British on the
sepoys who took part in it were often appalling. Executions without trial
were commonplace. The British victory in the Mutiny was tinged with
bitterness on both sides which lasted for several generations to come.

c) The Mutiny and the Historians

Not surprisingly, the Indian Mutiny has been the subject of heated
debate among historians. It was once traditional for Indian historians to
view the Mutiny as a national revolution against British rule. British
historians, on the other hand, viewed it as a localised army revolt
triggered off by the introduction of the Enfield rifle. In recent times,
both interpretations have been revised.

The classic Indian orthodox view can be found in *The Indian War of
Independence* by V.D. Savarkar (1912) who saw the Mutiny as a
nationalist uprising, the chief aim of which was to break free of British
rule. Many Indian historians have raised objections to this interpretation. For example, R.C. Majumdar views it as 'a sporadic revolt
triggered by religious zealots', and the term 'rebellion' is more
frequently used than 'revolution' in more recent Indian writings. The
Mutiny is being increasingly seen as backward looking, with the
muntineers focusing their dislike of British rule on the policy of
westernisation. Their main desire was not a new India but a restoration
of the cherished religious, social and economic traditions of the old one.
For S.R. Ghosh the Mutiny was the last gasp of the Mughal Empire
rather than the first flowering of Indian nationalism.

The classic British view of the Mutiny was put forward in *The
Cambridge History of the British Empire,* published in 1924. This
portrayed it as 'a series of localised outbursts within the army'. The main
facts presented to support this interpretation were that 66 per cent of the
country took no part, that only 25 per cent of the sepoys were involved,
that no outstanding leader of the mutiny emerged, and that there was no
planning or co-ordination. However, in more recent studies the broader
social and economic discontent over the policy of westernisation has
been given more emphasis, although the view that the Mutiny was a
'nationalist' revolt has been overwhelmingly rejected. C. Hibbert in *The*

Great Mutiny (1973) viewed it as something more than a 'Mutiny' but a good deal less than 'the first Indian war of independence'. In agreement with Ghosh, he saw it as 'the last swan song of Old India' - one last passionate protest against the penetration of the west. P. Mason, in *The Men Who Ruled India* (1955) saw it as 'inspired by people for whom progress was too fast', while Karl de Schweinitz in *The Rise and Fall of British India* (1983) interpreted it as the predictable reaction of a traditional agricultural society suddenly forced to accept the 'alien' disciplines of capitalism.

The result of all this work has been the adoption of a more balanced approach, although no consensus has as yet emerged. British historians generally now accept that the Mutiny had deeper causes than simple animosity over the introduction of the Enfield rifle, but they continue to reject the view that its aims were similar to the later Indian nationalist movement. For their part, Indian historians now generally acknowledge that the mutineers wanted to turn the clock back to the regionalised old India, rather than to create a nationally united new India.

d) The Results of the Mutiny

It is generally agreed that, whichever way it is interpreted, the Mutiny was a fundamental turning point in the history of British rule of India. It led to four important changes in the nature of British rule in India. Firstly, the involvement of the East India Company in the machinery of British rule was ended. Secondly, the Mutiny marks the beginning of total British rule. A Secretary of State and a council of 15 ministers was appointed to run Indian affairs. A Viceroy replaced the Governor-General as the new ruler of India. Thirdly, the British Indian army was reformed as a result of the Mutiny. The European element was strengthened, sepoys were not allowed to use heavy artillary weapons, and every two sepoy units was supervised by a British battalion. The British officer class treated sepoys with greater respect. The success of these reforms may be judged by the fact that between 1857 and 1947 there were no further large-scale mutinies in the army. The fourth, and the most significant result of the Mutiny was the adoption by the British government of a policy of appeasement which aimed to pacify the grievances of the power brokers of Old India. The Indian rulers of the 'princely states', who the British had sought to undermine before the Mutiny, had their prestige restored. They became an important collaborating group for the remainer of the period of British rule. All social, religious and cultural matters were left in their hands.

3 British Rule During the 'Golden Age of the Raj'

The success of these measures may be judged by the fact that the period from the end of the Mutiny to Queen Victoria's death in 1901 is usually dubbed the 'golden age of the British Raj'.

a) The Nature of British Rule

It is sometimes not fully realised that less than 3,000 British appointed officials ruled a vast sub-continent of nearly 300 million people. The British officials who ruled India were an educated elite. They gained their jobs through competitive examinations which were only held in London. Most of those who were appointed had attended British public schools and were 'the flower of the Universities' of Oxford and Cambridge. Sir John Strachey, a prominent British administrator, said in 1888 that British administrators of India 'ought to be Englishmen'. In 1914, 95 per cent of them were.

Nehru, the Indian Prime Minister from 1948 to 1965, observed that, 'the British in India were aloof, absorbed in their own concerns and tended to treat the Indian in a social or official capacity as a second class citizen and avoided close contact with Indians of any description'. This was not true of all British administrators. There was certainly an element among the British administrators who distanced themselves from Indian culture. Many only mixed socially with Indians on ceremonial occasions. Yet some British historians have shown that many British administrators were honest, well intentioned and often displayed empathy with India and its people.

Nevertheless, a prevailing feeling did exist among educated, English-speaking Indians that they were treated as second-class citizens by the British men who ruled India. As B.N. Pandey in *The Break-Up of British India* (1969) put it 'the racial arrogance of the British hurt the feelings of educated Indians and widened the gulf between ruler and ruled'. Many leading administrators displayed crude views of racial superiority. General Mayo, the Viceroy of India (1869-72) told a leading administrator that his major task while in India was to 'teach your subordinates that we are all British gentlemen engaged in the magnificent work of governing an inferior race'. This was not the whole story. There were many British 'Liberal' administrators, including Ripon and Hardinge who treated Indians as equals and made strong and well meaning efforts to ensure that crude views about racial superiority were discouraged among British administrators.

This did not prevent a large group of educated Indian professionals believing that they were denied equality of opportunity within the machinery of British rule. These professional men - teachers, lawyers, doctors, journalists and engineers - felt sufficiently strongly about this issue to found a nationalist movement which initially sought equal status for Indians, and eventually sought the end of British rule in India.

4 The Rise of Indian Nationalism

Indian nationalism was strongly influenced by the way in which nationalism was perceived by Europeans. But the European ideal of nationalism as a shared desire for self-government based on a common language, customs, and culture was a difficult concept for a regionalised and religiously divided society such as India to accommodate. The nationalist movement faced a number of difficulties in applying a European ideal of nationalism to Indian conditions.

The major religious division was between Hindus - the largest religious group (70 per cent) - and Muslims (21 per cent). The remaining religious groups (9 per cent), included Sikhs, Christians and Jews. Yet it was the Hindus who thought of themselves as the protectors of ancient India. All things foreign were seen as 'alien'. This view was reinforced by the fact that other religions - especially Islam, but also minority religions such as Christianity and Zorastianism - had been introduced by invaders. For example, the powerful Mughal Empire was a Muslim empire. The Mughals' dominance had ensured that the Muslim religion was an important part of Indian culture, but devout Hindus always remained loyal to their own religion as the 'true religion of the Indian people'.

Each Indian province had a distinct history, an ancient ruling dynasty, and local customs, laws, traditions, and language or languages. The vast majority of Indian people felt part of a distinct region of India and had no concept of India as a modern nation state. In fact, for most of them the idea of a nation with a central government, national laws, and national institutions was yet another 'alien' concept. These deep regional differences in Indian society would have to be overcome if nationalism was to stand any chance of winning widespread support.

Even if the nationalists were to be successful in overcoming the obstacles to winning mass support from the Indian population, they would still be faced by the British, who were in complete control of the sub-continent and who showed no sign of being prepared to share their power. This meant that Indian nationalism would clearly have to confront the British - either militarily, which was a daunting task, or by attempting to convince them by force of argument. The prospects of the nationalists were indeed bleak. Not surprisingly, Indian nationalism grew very slowly.

The beginning of Indian nationalism in an organised form was the establishment of the Indian Association in 1876. This pressure group of English-speaking, educated, Indian professionals demanded greater equality of opportunity for Indians employed in the Indian Civil Service. They held meetings and encouraged Indian scholarship and teaching. The British thought the group so harmless that in response to their demands they set up the Indian National Congress in 1885. This was designed as a powerless talking shop in which the Indian middle class would be able to air their grievances. The British never thought it would assume the status - as it eventually did - of an official opposition to British rule, and would become a national political party. The early meetings of the Congress gave the British little cause for concern. The speakers generally spent their time lauding the benefits that British rule had brought them. However, this timid beginning was soon followed by genuine debate, which tended to focus on criticisms of British rule. The Indian National Congress rapidly attracted the support of educated Indians. In 1900 each region had a local congress which sent delegates to the national congress.

The best known leaders of Congress before 1914 were Gokhale and Tilak. Gokhale admired British Liberalism. He was conciliatory and constructive in his criticisms of British rule. What he desired was the gradual introduction of local and national self-government for the Indian people along the same lines as had occurred in the settlement colonies. Rational argument, persuasion, and non-violence were central to his strategy. Tilak, on the other hand, was a devout Hindu. He admired the national heritage of India. He stressed how much of that heritage had been destroyed by British imperialism. Tilak favoured open and violent confrontation with the British. He wanted to force them out in an armed struggle - 'a national mutiny'. The British called the group led by Gokhale 'the moderates' and, not surprisingly, the group led by Tilak 'the extremists'.

Before 1900 the majority of the members of Congress supported the Gokhale approach towards the British. This all changed after George Nathaniel Curzon (Lord Curzon) - 'an imperialist heart and soul' - was appointed Viceroy of India in 1898.

5 Lord Curzon as Viceroy, 1898-1905

Lord Curzon was only 39 years old when he arrived in India. He was handsome, high minded and high handed in equal proportions. He had the self-confidence of someone who thought it was his divine right to lead. 'It is no good', he said, 'trusting a human being to do a thing for you. Do everything yourself.'

Curzon looked upon his period as Viceroy of India as a mere stepping stone to becoming leader of the Unionist Party and Prime Minister. This was not misplaced ambition. He was viewed as the rising star on the imperialist right. His passion for British rule in India was as strong as Romeo's had been for Juliet. He was so patriotic he even refused to have the hymn 'Onward Christian Soldiers' sung during church services in India because it contained the lines: 'Crowns and thrones may perish, Kingdoms rise and wane'.

Lord Curzon believed that Britain was in India to stay. Not surprisingly, this meant he was extremely hostile towards the rising influence of the Indian National Congress. In 1900 he said, 'my own belief is that the Congress is tottering to its fall and one of my greatest ambitions while in India is to assist it to a peaceful demise'. Curzon ruled India in the style of a Roman Emperor. His arrivals in India were legendary for their display of imperial pomp and ceremony. The wife of a Bengal civilian described one of these glittering parades.

> 1 First, mounted police, then five regiments of cavalry, then artillery, then the heralds, grand in yellow and gold, blowing a fanfare as they reached the mosque. After them, the Imperial Cadets, a corps of young natives, sons of noblemen, all mounted on black chargers
> 5 with leopard skins, and dressed in white uniforms and pale blue turbans - they were really lovely! And then came the elephants ... and it was just a dazzling procession, one more splendid than another ... Six came together, first, three and three ... then a splendid creature covered with silver and gold and carrying a
> 10 howdah in which sat Lord Curzon and his lovely lady ... they came slowly and majestically along, followed by a train of forty or fifty magnificent animals, all decked and painted and bedizened with cloth of gold and dazzling frontlet pieces and great hanging ornaments over their ears ... But there was hardly any noise and no
> 15 cheering to speak of.

It was only while he was aboard an elephant that Curzon ever moved slowly during his whole period as Viceroy. His aim while in India was to enact an ambitious programme of administrative and economic reform which would keep Britain in India 'for at least another hundred years'. He set up a series of national departments with seperate responsibility for land, research, railways, and agriculture. He improved road, rail and river transport. He encouraged greater British investment.

Curzon's policies in general were very unpopular among educated Indians, but it was his decision to partition the ancient province of Bengal into two regions which caused a nationalist outcry among the population at large. Bengal, predominantly Hindu with a population of 78 million, was the largest Indian province with a clear regional identity which its people were willing to defend. When he decided to partition Bengal, Curzon had looked at the question purely in terms of administrative efficiency. He believed the province was too large and unwieldy to be governed effectively without a division into two separate units.

Not surprisingly, the people of Bengal viewed the matter somewhat differently. They interpreted it as as a direct attack by the British on the ancient regional boundaries of India. With the support of the National Congress, a British administrative reform with local implications was translated into a national issue. The Congress led the protests through speeches, street demonstrations, and a boycott of British manufactured goods. Terrorist attacks against British administrators also took place.

The main theme of the nationalist attack was that the British had shown once more, as they had prior to the Mutiny, they had little respect for Indian customs, religious practices or ancient regional loyalties. A regional issue was thus translated into a national revolt.

A great many Indian historians have viewed the partition of Bengal as the birthplace of a full-blown nationalist movement. The Congress was able to spread fears that other ancient Indian provinces might face the same fate as Bengal unless they took a stand against British rule. The crisis was undoubtedly important in raising the profile of Congress as a group capable of providing leadership for the Indian people. The crisis led to the formation of the All Indian Muslim League which also fought against British rule by violent means. These two developments were clearly something all Curzon's efforts had been designed to avoid. The view that the partition was a politically significant event in the history of British rule remains persuasive, especially as the Bengal affair also led to the demise of Lord Curzon who was the last truly visionary and 'imperial' Viceroy of India. When the Liberals returned to power in 1905 they quickly replaced Curzon with the far more conciliatory Lord Minto.

6 The Liberals and India, 1905-14

The victory of the Liberals in the British general election of 1906 was greeted with enthusiasm by the leading members of the Congress. The moderates in the Congress were great admirers of the 'fair-mindedness of British Liberalism' and had high hopes that Morley, the Secretary of State for India, would move India along the path towards self-government. Yet Minto, the Liberal Viceroy, viewed self-government for India as 'a fantastic, ludicrous, dream'. However, unlike Curzon, he did take Congress seriously, consulted it about the possibility of reform.

Between 1905 and 1914 the Liberal government introduced several important reforms affecting India. These reforms were clearly a response to the nationalist demand for greater involvement by Indians in the machinery of British rule. The Indian Councils Act (1909) allowed elected Indian representatives to sit on the Legislative Council of the Viceroy in India, the Council for India in London, and on the previously British-dominated local legislative councils. The Imperial Council was turned into a legislature with 27 of its 60 members being elected rather than appointed by the Viceroy. There was no in-built British majority on this council. Direct elections were introduced for local council elections. Separate representative councils were also offered to Muslims.

Lord Hardinge, who replaced Minto as Viceroy in 1910, further eased tension by re-uniting Bengal. He also developed very close relations with Gokhale and the moderates in the Congress. These contacts led to the Islington Commission in 1912. This recommended that 'Indianisation' of the Higher Civil service should be made a key future priority of British rule in India.

The Liberal Reforms in India from 1905 to 1914 did ease the tension created by the partition of Bengal, but they were no more than a tentative beginning to finding a solution to the problem of British rule in India. And there was still the need to deal with the All Indian Muslim League, which was promoting terrorism and civil disorder. In 1914 the British were still in command, but they had not answered the most important nationalist question of all - when would self-government for India be granted? The First World War began before they were required to supply an answer.

7 British Policy in the Rest of Asia

The main aim of British policy in the rest of Asia was to expand British trade and commerce. The power of the Royal Navy was crucial for this purpose. Most of the major Far-Eastern trading centres - apart from those in Japan - were either 'persuaded' or forced to accept foreign goods. This was known as the 'open door' policy. It was used most successfully to open up Chinese ports.

a) The 'Open Door Policy' and Anglo-Chinese Relations

Britain was interested in China because of its huge potential as a market for British goods. As Lord Palmerston said in 1864, 'what must be the commercial advantage to this country if it can have unimpeded and uninterrupted commerce with one third of the human race'. Yet this fascination with 'opening up China' was out of all proportion to the actual volume of Anglo-Chinese trade. In any one year during the nineteenth century imports from China never rose above £2.5 million and exports to China were never higher than £5.5 million. In spite of the 'open door' policy, Anglo-Chinese trade never made up more than 1 per cent of total British overseas trade at any time between 1815 and 1914. But, of course, it was the prospects for future growth rather than the current reality that caused such interest among British traders.

The main reason trade links with China by European powers grew so slowly was the isolationist policies pursued by the Chinese government. The Manchu dynasty, which had ruled China since the seventeenth century, followed a consistent policy of attempting to isolate its empire from western trade, western ideas, and western influence. China was viewed as 'the centre of the universe', which had no need of contact with those outside its borders. Before 1842 China signed no diplomatic or trade agreements with any European power.

China was able to resist the penetration of the west for so long because her economy was self-sufficient in all vital foods and raw materials, and her army of one million men was considered the strongest in Asia. Until about 1880 European powers looked on China as a major power, comparable to Russia, and none seriously contemplated risking a land war with her. However, the Manchu dynasty spent very little on its naval defences. This offered Britain - the world's strongest naval power - the chance to force China to open its ports to foreign trade. The Royal Navy blockaded Chinese ports in order to force China to accept foreign goods.

The policy was first used to support the trading activities of the East India Company. Early in the nineteenth century the export of the drug opium, from India to the Chinese port of Canton, had become vital to the profitability of the East India Company. In 1800 China banned the sale of opium. This was a serious blow for the East India Company. It responded by selling the drug to Indian merchants who smuggled it illegally into China.

The desire of the British to trade and the reluctance of China to allow them to do so eventually led to a naval war between Britain and China. In 1839 the Chinese government seized and destroyed all foreign stocks of opium. The drug smugglers were given the death penalty. At Canton the number of drug raids on foreign vessels was increased. The East India Company called on the British government for help. Ships of the Royal Navy were sent to Canton to mount a blockade. This resulted in a naval skirmish between Chinese junks and the Royal Navy during which two British ships and four Chinese war junks were sunk.

The incident was used by the British government to escalate the dispute into a war. From 1839 to 1842 all the major Chinese ports were blockaded. This action became known as the 'Opium War'. It was carried out for the narrow purpose of aiding the trade of the East India Company and for the broader purpose of forcing the Chinese government to open up its ports to foreign trade. In 1842 China gave in and signed the Treaty of Nanking. Despite the fact that the British government declared that its aim in fighting the war was 'trade not territory', China was compelled to cede the island of Hong Kong to Britain, as well as to pay her a £13 million indemnity, to open five ports to British merchants, and to reduce the import duty on British goods to 5 per cent. But even this did not satisfy British and European traders. The Chinese government only allowed them to operate within a 30 mile radius of the five 'open-door' ports. Of these only Shanghai became a truly international city. The vast majority of China still remained free of foreign trade. Between 1856 and 1858 a second 'trade war' was fought - this time with French co-operation. This led to five more Chinese ports being opened to foreign trade.

The 'open-door' policy was successful in economic terms for Britain. In 1880 she was responsible for 76 per cent of all Chinese overseas trade. But it is questionable whether China benefited from it. Centuries of seclusion from western ideas and influence were ended, but the illusion of Chinese power was shattered and the country was left vulnerable to the ambitions of Britain, France, Germany, Russia and Japan.

b) The 'New Imperialism in Asia': China and the European Powers

The growing realisation that China was in a weak condition encouraged other European powers to seek rich pickings in Asia. In the 1880s France arrived in Indo-China, capturing Tonking, Cambodia and Saigon. The British responded to the French threat by taking formal control of Burma, Malaya and Borneo. Germany and the USA also arrived to take control of several Pacific Islands. Japan and Russia were also interested in expansion.

This wave of 'new imperialism' in Asia nearly led to the European powers partitioning China. The naval attacks aimed at enforcing the 'open-door' policy were followed by military attacks. In 1860 Russia attacked China and annexed a large amount of territory near the Amur River. This allowed Russia to build the ice-free naval base of Vladivostock. In 1894 Japan, the most rapidly advancing independent Asian power, attacked and defeated China. As the price of victory Japan demanded large amounts of territory. This alarmed Britain, Russia, Germany and France, who intervened diplomatically. In the end Japan accepted a £30 million war indemnity. But China could not pay. This opened the way for European banks to lend money to China in return for mineral rights, railway contracts, and land.

The European powers began to view China as a 'dying' power in a world where only the fittest were destined to survive. In 1898 Germany captured the port of Kiao-Chow, Britain took Wei-hai-wei, and the Russians grabbed Port Arthur. In 1900 China, historically the most powerful and influential state in Asia, was perilously close to partition; so close that Germany, France, Britain, and Russia had already drawn up plans to ensure that the division of the spoils would be carried out peacefully. The *Times,* which was known as 'the voice of the British Government', summed up the prevailing view of China's sorry plight in 1898 when it suggested that any attempt to prevent a partition of China would be like 'trying to keep the ocean out with a mop'.

However, the Chinese were not prepared to give up their independence without a struggle. In 1900, with partition imminent, large numbers of Chinese nationalists rose up and attacked Europeans wherever they were to be found. This was 'The Boxer Rebellion'. Many Europeans and many more Chinse rebels were killed before Germany, France, Russia and Britain intervened, suppressed the rebellion, and restored order.

In the end China was only saved from partition because the European powers feared the ambitions of each other more than they wanted to rule China. They finally agreed to accept a partition of trading concessions in

China. Russia took control of trade in the north (including Peking), France gained exclusive trading rights in the South, and Germany gained concessions in Shantung. This left Britain with the Yangtse valley - the most important trading region of all. But as Britain had previously controlled over 70 per cent of all Chinese foreign trade this was hardly a completely satisfactory outcome. What did satisfy Britain was the survival of an independent China. This was what British diplomacy had been aiming at all along.

8 The End of 'Splendid Isolation' in Asia, 1900-14

Yet for how long could Britain go on winning these delicate games of international diplomacy? How long could Britain on her own hold back the tide of great power ambitions in Asia? After 1900 politicians began to think that the answer to both questions was 'not for very long'. The feverish imperial rivalry in Africa and Asia had stretched Britain's naval and military resources to the limit. Germany and the USA had emerged as major economic and naval rivals. Russia was thought to remain a real threat to India. The presence of France in Indo-China and the growing militarism of Japan suggested that uncertainties would increase in the future.

The vulnerability of the Empire in Asia was often the subject of discussion among leading British politicians. The debate centred on the desirability of continuing with 'splendid isolation', the policy of Britain joining no military alliances. Lord Salisbury, the Prime Minister, supported it on the grounds that it gave Britain 'no friends and yet no enemies'. There were others who wanted Britain to abandon the policy and enter an alliance - 'with anyone'. Joseph Chamberlain, the Colonial Secretary, flirted with the idea of an Anglo-German alliance. But the animosity between Britain and Germany increased - mainly over naval rivalry - and by 1902 all hopes of an alliance between the two countries had evaporated.

The costly Anglo-Boer War in South Africa (1899-1902) quickened the desire of the British government to sign diplomatic agreements in order to end what seemed to be an increasingly dangerous isolation. It was recognised that had another international crisis arisen while the war in South Africa was being fought, there would have been insufficient available forces to deal with it. The first agreement was with an Asian power - Japan. The aim of this was to offer the prospect of assistance in any war Britain became involved in in the Far East, thereby reducing the worry about having insufficient resources in the region to defend British interests in all circumstances. It was also hoped that the mere existence of the Anglo-Japanese treaty would deter potential aggressors from taking action. Yet its first result was to encourage Japan to go to war with Russia in 1904 in a dispute over the control of north-east China. The Russo-Japanese War ended in 1905 in a surprising Japanese victory.

It was clear the Anglo-Japanese alliance had done little to ease the tension in Asia. Two other agreements were more successful in this respect. In 1904 the Anglo-French entente was signed. This settled British differences with France over colonial matters in Africa and Asia. In 1907 Britain and Russia finally settled their bitter colonial differences in Asia by signing the Anglo-Russian Convention. Border disputes over Afghanistan and Tibet were resolved, and Persia (now Iran) was divided into British and Russian 'spheres of influence', with a 'neutral' zone in between.

However, these agreements did not solve all Britain's difficulties in Asia. It seemed that any new challenge to her interests in the region might reveal that the military and naval resources needed to mount an effective response were lacking. The British Empire had flourished in times of peace, but had definitely become overstretched when serious imperial rivals appeared on the scene. India appeared to be in a particularly vulnerable position, given that any external aggressor was likely to receive support from dissidents within the sub-continent. One beneficial effect for Britain of the outbreak of war in 1914 was that it focused the attention of the major powers on Europe just at a time when the problem of defending the Empire had became a major issue, and before the word 'decline' had seriously been contemplated for the British Empire in Asia.

Making notes on *'The British Empire in Asia, 1815-1914'*

Questions on the British Empire in Asia usually centre on three issues: i) the causes and consequences of the Indian Mutiny, ii) the rise of Indian nationalism between 1880 and 1914, and iii) Britain's relations with China. It would be a good idea to keep this in mind as you make your notes.

1   The Mutiny. Pay close attention to the developments which led to the Mutiny. What was the significance of the policy of westernisation? List the characteristics of the policy and the reactions of the Indians to it. Pay particular attention to the historical debate and list examples of British and Indian perspectives.

2   The Rise of Indian Nationalism. Note the consequences of the Mutiny for British rule. What were the differences between the nationalism of the Mutiny and the 'new nationalism'? What problems faced any Indian nationalist movement? Take notes on the aims, tactics and leadership of the National Congress. What was the significance for the growth of the Indian nationalist movement of Curzon as Viceroy and of the period of Liberal reforms from 1905 to 1914?

3   Britain's Relations with China. Why was China vulnerable to external aggressors during the nineteenth century? What was the

'open-door' policy? What were the causes and consequences of the Opium War? Describe and explain Britain's response to each of the threats made to Chinese independence.

Answering essay questions on '*The British Empire in Asia, 1815-1914*'

Study the following questions on the British Empire in Asia.

1 Was the Indian Mutiny the 'last gasp of Old India'?
2 'A nationalist revolt'. How valid is this description of the Indian Mutiny?
3 Explain why Indian nationalism grew in the years from 1880 to 1914.
4 Account for the rise of the Indian National Congress between 1870 and 1914.
5 Was the 'open-door' policy towards China a classic case of 'informal imperialism'?

One of the advantages of studying this topic is that examiners tend to set self-contained questions on it. You are therefore unlikely to find yourself frustrated by the appearance of a question that links an aspect of the British Empire in Asia with a topic you know little about. You will notice

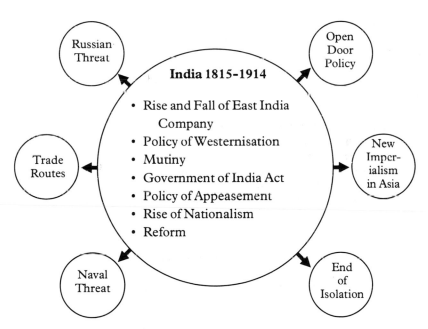

Summary - The British Empire in Asia, 1815-1914

that four of the questions on page 69 are completely self-contained, while only one requires you to consider an issue in a wider context. Which question is the exception to the 'self-contained' rule?

Another advantage of being prepared to answer questions on the British Empire in Asia is that examiners often set a straightforward task, as is frequently the case when it is considered probable that even well-prepared candidates will possess relatively little factual knowledge about the topic. Two of the questions are essentially of the simple 'why?' type, requiring no more than a sequence of 'because' points sandwiched between an introduction and a conclusion. Which are the questions that fall into this category? When you come to prepare plans for answers to these questions, remember that the 'because' points should not be presented in random order. What criterion will you use to decide on the order you will adopt?

Questions 1, 2, and 5 demand a similar range of essay-writing skills of the candidate. What is the common factor? Question 5 is the most difficult in terms of technique, but it is quite manageable as long as it is approached systematically. The first task is to identify the terms or concepts that need to be defined. In this case there are three of them - 'open-door' policy', 'classic case', and 'informal imperialism'. If you are confident that you will be able to construct a definition of each term, it will be worth your while continuing with the question. If you are not, now is the time to switch to another question. Your next task is to think out your definitions. In an examination situation, with time at a premium, it would be best to do this by writing the introductory section of your answer. Because there are three definitions to give, with two of them being lengthy, you will probably need more than one introductory paragraph - this situation rarely arises, but it is by no means unique. When you have done this you need to stop writing and do some more planning. Your task now is to think out the rest of your answer. There are two stages to this. First you need to study the wording of the question and identify exactly what it is that you are being asked to do. In this case the examiner is looking for a 'in these respects, yes, in these respects, no' answer. Then you need to decide what your 'yes' and 'no' points will be and the order in which you will present them. Once this has been done, writing the answer should be straightforward!

Most students are likely to find the previous paragraph very daunting. This is not to be wondered at because it presents a tough challenge. However, given that you have bothered to read this section thus far, it is probable that you will have the sticking-power to practise your essay-planning technique sufficiently rigorously to be able (eventually) to handle the approach that has been described. Certainly, students with good planning techniques almost invariably achieve significantly better results than those who do nearly all their thinking as they write.

Source-based questions on 'The British Empire in Asia, 1815-1914'

1 The Orders to a British Officer during the Indian Mutiny
Carefully read the extract on page 56. Answer the following questions.
a) What are the orders being given in the extract? (3 marks)
b) What does the extract tell us about the attitude of the British officers to the mutineers? (3 marks)
c) Explain the strengths and weaknesses of the source for the military historian. (4 marks)

2 A British Officer's Evidence from Cawnpore
Carefully read the extract on page 57. Answer the following questions.
a) What is the officer's attitude towards the mutineers? Back up each of your points with evidence from the extract. (6 marks)
b) What conclusions about the nature of the conflict can be drawn from the extract? (4 marks)
c) What other types of evidence are likely to be available to allow a judgement to be made about whether what happened at Cawnpore was typical of the Mutiny as a whole? (5 marks)

3 An Indian View of British Rule
Carefully read the extract on page 62. Answer the following questions.
a) Explain briefly what is being described in the extract. (3 marks)
b) What does the extract suggest about the style of British rule at the time? (3 marks)
c) What is the significance of the the fact that, despite the impressive display of British power, 'there was hardly any noise and no cheering to speak of'? (4 marks)

CHAPTER 5

The Empire, British Politics and Popular Culture in the Age of Imperialism

In recent years historians have devoted a great deal of attention to the impact of the Empire on British politics and society. After 1870 the Empire became a major issue of debate in political circles. An increased interest in the Empire among the working class and within popular forms of entertainment and literature was also apparent. The process began in the 1870s with a major debate over the future of the Empire between Benjamin Disraeli, the Conservative leader, and William Gladstone, the Liberal leader. By the 1890s Joseph Chamberlain, 'the uncrowned king of the imperialists', had come forward with plans for the 'expansion of the Empire'. The climax of all this imperial excitement was reached in the Anglo-Boer War (1899-1902).

1 Disraeli and the Empire

Benjamin Disraeli (1804-81) led the Conservative Party in the Commons for much of the time from 1846 until his death in 1881. He was Prime Minister twice, in 1868 and between 1874 and 1880. But his greatest creation was his own controversial personality which has been the subject of disagreement ever since. Robert Blake suggests his major contribution was to create for the Conservatives the image of a national and patriotic party, rising above class loyalties to represent the British people as a whole. Yet among his contemporaries he was viewed as an 'unprincipled opportunist' who took up issues for reasons of personal advancement and in order to increase his popularity. It is easy to see why this view was held. Throughout his career Disraeli frequently changed his stance. When he tried to enter parliament for the first time he stood, in turn, as a Whig, a Radical, and finally as a Tory. He opposed electoral reform in 1832 and then supported it in 1867. He opposed free trade in 1846 only to make it Conservative policy in 1852. He called the colonies 'millstones around our necks' in the 1860s, but in the 1870s was calling for the 'consolidation of the Empire'.

Equal scepticism has been raised about the reasons why Disraeli suddenly injected the issue of Empire into British domestic politics. The starting point was his speech at Crystal Palace in 1872 when he said of Liberal policy towards the Empire,

1 If you look at the history of this country since the advent of Liberalism - forty years ago - you will find there has been no effort so continuous, so subtle, supported by so much energy and carried

out with so much ability and acumen, as the attempts of Liberalism
5 to effect the disintegration of the Empire of England. And,
gentlemen, of all its efforts, this is the one which has been the
nearest to success. It has been shown that there has never been a
Jewel in the crown of England that was so truly costly as the
possession of India. How often has it been suggested that we
10 should at once emancipate ourselves from this costly incubus.
Well, that result was very nearly accomplished. When those subtle
views were adopted by the country under the plausible idea of
granting self-government to the colonies ... Not that I for one
object to self-government. I cannnot conceive how our distant
15 colonies can have their affairs administered except by self-
government. But self-government in my opinion, when it was
conceded, ought to have been conceded as part of a great policy of
imperial consolidation ... It ought further, to have been
accompanied by the institution of some representative council in
20 the metropolis, which would have brought the colonies into
constant and continuous relations with the Home Government.
All this, however, was omitted, because those who advised that
policy looked even upon our connection with India, as a burden to
this country, viewed everything in its financial aspect, and totally
25 ignoring those moral and political considerations which make
nations great, and by influence of which alone men are
distinguished from animals. In my opinion no minister in this
country will do his duty who neglects any opportunity of
reconstructing as much as possible our colonial empire.

The front line of Disraeli's attack against the Liberals in the Crystal
Palace speech was on their handling of policy towards India. As Prime
Minister between 1874 and 1880 he put the consolidation of British
power in India, the trade of India and the defence of India at the heart of
his imperial crusade. In 1875 he purchased the Khedive of Egypt's 41
per cent share holding in the Suez Canal Company. This demonstrated
a firm British committment towards defending the shortest trade route
to India. In 1876 he arranged for Queen Victoria to assume the title of
'Empress of India'. This emphasised a firm commitment towards British
imperial rule.

The strongly anti-Russian tone in Disraeli's foreign policy emphasised a determination to defend India from Tsarist ambitions. Russia was
thought to pose the greatest threat to Indian security, both as a potential
aggressor via Afghanistan and as a menacer of the middle-eastern
portion of the route between Britain and India. In the heated discussion
of the Eastern Question, Disraeli supported the 'ailing' Ottoman
Empire - the 'sick man of Europe'. The Eastern Question revolved
around what the great powers would do in the event of the collapse of
the Ottoman Empire. Disraeli believed that an Ottoman collapse would

benefit Russia and thereby threaten India. In 1876, when the Turks massacred thousands of Christians in Bulgaria, Disraeli refused, with Queen Victoria's blessing, to condemn the Turks. In 1877 when Russia declared war on Turkey, Disraeli gave diplomatic support to the Turks. In the face of British pressure, Russia backed down. In 1878 Russia settled, briefly, her differences with Turkey at the Congress of Berlin. Although this tough anti-Russian policy had brought Britain to the verge of war, Disraeli was unrepentant about the stand he had taken, and his actions seemed vindicated on his return from Berlin where he was greeted as a national hero who had gained 'peace with honour' - as well as acquiring Cyprus as his reward for supporting the Turks.

Jingoism, the vociferous support by the masses of the defence of British interests abroad, was the term used by contemporaries to explain this new popular phenomenon. The word 'jingo' came from a popular music hall song of the period called 'By Jingo' which contained the words,

> We don't want to fight but by jingo if we do
> We've got ships, we've got the men
> We've got the money too.
> We've fought the bear [Russia] before, and while Britons true
> The Russians shall not have Constantinople.

However, there is good reason to believe that Disraeli's Indian obsession and the popular jingoism it encouraged were matters of political style rather than of political substance. When what he did (rather than what he said) is considered it is possible to understand why many historians have reached the conclusion that Disraeli's championing of imperialism was mainly show. There were no new administrative or economic policies for the Empire enacted by Disraeli as Prime Minister. Despite all his talk at Crystal Palace about the misguided Liberal decision to offer self-government to the colonies of settlement, he completely ignored the colonies of settlement when he was in power. In fact, it seems that he virtually ignored the Empire as a whole. All the major decisions on imperial policy were left to the Earl of Carnarvon, the Colonial Secretary, who had no desire for an expansionist policy. No increases were made in government spending on the Empire or on imperial defence under Disraeli. Even during the instances of active British military intervention in defence of the Empire, including Fiji (1875), Transvaal (1879), Afghanistan (1879), and the Zulu War (1879) there is no evidence of an active role being played by Disraeli.

Typical of those who have accused Disraeli of being a sham imperialist is C.C. Eldridge who, in *Victorian Imperialism* (1977), suggested that beneath the rhetoric there was nothing new in Disraeli's policy towards the Empire. However, this 'negative' line of interpretation has not ever been universally accepted. For example, Robert Blake in *Disraeli* (1966) took a different view. He suggested that

Disraeli's opportunism towards the Empire had an underlying purpose. This was to associate the Conservative Party with patriotism in order to make a new appeal to the electorate for the underlying and principle aim of defending the Empire.

2 Gladstone and the Empire

William Ewart Gladstone (1809-98) was the dominant British politician of the nineteenth century. He won four general elections and became forever associated with the type of 'high-minded' Liberalism which is summed up in the phrase 'peace, retrenchment and reform'. He was so disgusted with the British public for electing Disraeli in 1874 that he resigned his parliamentary seat and retired to his country estate at Hawarden in North Wales. But he became so alarmed at Disraeli's 'jingoism' that he emerged from retirement and looked around for a by-election which would allow him to return to parliament. A vacancy in the Conservative-held Scottish constituency of Midlothian arose. Gladstone announced his candidacy and went on a whistle-stop speaking tour of Scotland, which became known as the Midlothian Campaign. This was the first example of modern campaigning in British politics.

The whole campaign was a bitter party political attack against Disraeli's 'imperialist ambitions'. In one speech Gladstone attacked Disraeli's decision to purchase the Suez Canal shares.

1 What is the meaning of safeguarding the road to India? It seems to
  mean this; that a little island at the end of the world, having
  possession of an enormous territory at the other end of the world, is
  entitled to say with respect to every land and every sea lying
5 between its shores and any part of that enormous possession, that it
  has a preferential right to the possession or control of that
  intermediate territory, in order, as it is called, to safe-guard the
  road to India. That, gentlemen, is a monstrous claim.

In other speeches, Gladstone accused Disraeli of conducting a 'sinister foreign policy, deliberately designed to stifle liberty and progress', and of inflaming the British public to display 'unworthy emotions' such as 'lust for glory, aggressiveness, and chauvinism'. He argued that the only way to counteract this 'slide towards imperialism' was to increase the ability of the Empire to defend itself, to champion the cause of peace, and to avoid needless and entangling engagements throughout the Empire.

The Midlothian Campaign was a *tour de force* for Gladstone and helped the Liberal Party win a sweeping victory at the 1880 general election. Gladstone portrayed the election as a triumph for the party of 'justice, moderation and peace over the party of aggression, intrigue and lawless national vanity'. However, the swift return of Gladstone as

Prime Minister, on his own personal crusade, aroused widespread criticism among many of those he had previously led. This is not surprising as he had not consulted the existing Liberal Party leadership over the campaign. In addition, the personal nature of the attack on Disraeli alarmed many inside his party, while a large number of radical MPs felt that the rising tide of social radicalism within the Liberal Party would be held back by Gladstone's unbending moderation. Outside his own party the critics were even more vociferous. The Conservative Party hailed Disraeli as a national hero who had restored British pride and promised to carry on his crusade to 'save the Empire'. Queen Victoria viewed Gladstone as a 'dangerous revolutionary'. Jingoism did not simply fade away.

After 1880 Gladstone and his particular brand of high-minded Liberalism was under attack. This forced him into a number of U-turns in imperial policy beteen 1880 and 1885. The most dramatic of these was his decision to order a British occupation of Egypt in 1882. This dealt a body blow to his policy of non-intervention and seemed to contradict the high moral principles which, during the Midlothian Campaign, he had said would be the basis of Liberal policy.

The way Gladstone handled the defence of Egypt forced him into another humiliating U-turn. Having occupied Egypt in 1882, Britain was forced to defend the country. One element of this was the defence of Egyptian forces in the Sudan. These troops became threatened when an extremist Muslim religious leader, Mohammed Ahmed who was known as the Mahdi, led a rising against the Egyptian occupation based at Khartoum. Rather than becoming embroiled in a war to defeat the Mahdi, Gladstone decided to evacuate the Egyptian forces. The man chosen for the task was Major-General Gordon who was a fervent imperialist and something of a religious zealot himself. Although Gordon's own forces were outnumbered, he refused to withdraw and his men became cut off. After much dithering, Gladstone decided to send a relief force to save Gordon. But, only two days before it finally arrived, General Gordon was killed in January 1885 when Khartoum was overrun by the Mahdi's men. The country was shocked by the death of 'Gordon of Khartoum' who became a hero figure among the imperialists. The public blamed his death on the indecision of Gladstone. He was held responsible for delaying the sending of a relief force with such tragic results for General Gordon.

The public reaction to the fiasco at Khartoum showed how much passion for imperialism was developing in Britain. But Gladstone was not in sympathy with it. By 1885 he was out of touch with the times and losing his touch as a politician. Newspapers such as the *Times* and the *Daily Telegraph* and periodicals such as the *Spectator* and *Punch* now turned sharply away from Gladstonian Liberalism. Large sections of the business community switched their financial support away from the Liberal Party and boosted the party funds of the Conservatives. A growing number of imperialists in Gladstone's own party were on the verge of revolt.

The question of Home Rule for Ireland was the issue which finally split the Liberal Party. Gladstone had tried to improve the condition of the Irish peasantry through Church and land reforms while Prime Minister from 1868 to 1874. These initiatives did not 'pacify' Ireland. Instead, they helped encourage the growth of an Irish nationalist movement led by Charles Stewart Parnell which demanded 'Home Rule For Ireland'. In 1886 Gladstone decided to introduce a Home Rule Bill. This decision left him open to the charge that what he granted to Ireland today would be granted to India and the other colonies tomorrow. The imperialists feared that Home Rule for Ireland would lead to the break up of the Empire. In this way the Irish home rule issue became linked with Gladstone's supposed anti-imperialism. In spite of the obvious dangers for the unity of the Liberal party, Gladstone decided to fight the 1886 election on the issue of Home Rule for Ireland. This decision produced a disastrous split within the Liberal Party. Over 50 Liberal MPs, including the radical and imperialist Joseph Chamberlain, formed a separate Unionist group. The Unionists and the Conservatives at first formed an electoral pact - and gained an overwhelming victory in the 1886 election - and then worked increasingly closely in parliament. By 1895 the Unionists had effectively become a part of the Conservative Party.

Despite the disastrous consequences of his Irish policy, Gladstone carried on as Liberal leader and continued to champion Home Rule. Even the fall of Parnell from the leadership of the Irish Nationalists over a messy divorce case in the late 1880s did not deter him. In 1892, when Gladstone took office for the last time, he was no longer a leader of opinion but was a prisoner of more powerful forces. His fourth government (1892-4) depended on the votes of the Irish Nationalist MPs and contained a growing group of 'Liberal imperialists' led by Lord Rosebery. Gladstone introduced a second Home Rule bill (this was rejected by the House of Lords). In 1894 Gladstone finally retired. A year later the Conservatives and Unionists gained a sweeping electoral victory. In 1898, before the high tide of imperialism was reached in the Boer War, Gladstone died.

Richard Shannon in the *Crisis of Imperialism* (1977) has argued that Gladstone was, at heart, a domestic politician whose views were anti-imperialist and non-interventionist. His contention is that the Liberal leader thought British greatness was based on her trade, her industry and her parliamentary institutions - not her Empire. He had little enthusiasm for colonial expansion and felt that a desire for national self-determination was an 'unquenchable thirst' of all peoples. He argued that Gladstone saw the Empire in largely economic terms - as a trading empire. This may explain why he so admired the self-governing colonies which he felt were a model which all the other colonies should aspire to follow. Contrary to popular myth, he had no intention of abandoning India. He accepted it as a fact of life and was prepared to defend it from rival powers. His main desire for India was that,

> nothing may bring about a sudden violent or discreditable severance; that we may labour steadily to promote the political training of our fellow subjects so that when we go, if we are to go, we may leave a clear bill of accounts behind us.

Despite all he had said at Midlothian, the Empire actually expanded far more rapidly under Gladstone than under Disraeli. The ground rules for the Scramble for Africa were laid by his government at the Berlin Conference (1884). Nevertheless, it is worth pointing out that very few British territorial gains made under his leadership were planned or desired. He chose to call British gains in Africa and Asia 'protectorates'. It appears this is what he genuinely believed most of them were. He wanted to protect both British 'interests' abroad and weaker powers from the strong. This helps to make sense of why he so often submerged his belief in non-intervention and his support for 'all nations struggling to be free' in the face of pressure from officials in the Colonial and Foreign Offices and from British colonial administrators abroad. Gladstone was a leader on most issues, but when it came to the Empire he was more often than not a follower of 'experts'.

3 Joseph Chamberlain: the Uncrowned King of the Imperialists?

As the Gladstonian era ended the imperialist era dawned. Its most influential champion was Joseph Chamberlain (1836-1914), who was born in London but who made his business fortune and his political name in Birmingham. As Lord Mayor of Birmingham in 1873 he implemented a wide-ranging programme of social reforms, including the clearing of slums, the provision of gas, water and toilets to homes that did not have them, and the building of schools, libraries and art galleries. These reforms became popularly known as 'Gas and Water Socialism'. He was a severe critic of Gladstone over Ireland, the Empire and social reform, and left the Liberal Party in 1886 over the issue of Home Rule for Ireland. He was Colonial Secretary in the Unionist government from 1895 to 1903, when he resigned from the Cabinet in order to form the Tariff Reform League. This fought to secure the adoption of protectionism as official Unionist Party policy. He had a stroke in 1906 and thereafter took very little active part in politics.

Joseph Chamberlain has been described as 'the most significant politician of the late-Victorian era'. Yet he never led a major political party, never became Prime Minister, and none of his grand schemes - for Tariff Reform, for a United Empire, and for social reform - were ever implemented. His major biographers - Judd, Browne, Balfour, and Amery - have used flattering phrases such as 'an extraordinary man of action', 'a dynamic imperialist', and 'a politician whose influence is crucial in understanding Britain's decline as a great power', to describe him. But Joseph Chamberlain has also correctly been viewed as one of the great might-have-beens of British politics, a politician who flitted from policy to policy, idea to idea, and party to party without ever achieving anything of substance.

The passion Joseph Chamberlain had for the future of the Empire was all consuming. He saw the retention of the Empire as a 'matter of life and death' for Britain. The expansion of the USA westward across America after 1860 convinced him that the great powers of the twentieth century would be those with large territory and great natural resources - not a small island with a large navy. He considered that the only way for Britain to avoid decline was by action to consolidate and expand the Empire into a sort of United States of Empire. In his speeches he constantly stressed the need for a new direction in policy towards the Empire.

1 The Imperial idea has only recently taken root in this country. We
  have only to look back to the lifetime of many of us to remember a
  period of apathy and indifference, in which our statesmen were
  eager chiefly to rid themselves of responsibility and felt that home
5 affairs were as much as they could properly be called upon to
  attend to. At that time our colonies were crying out for our
  sympathy. Now we have gone ahead; now, I think we are perhaps
  in advance of our colonies. The new conception of Empire is of a
  voluntary organisation based on community of interests and
10 community of sacrifices to which all should bring their
  contribution to the common good. It is this new spirit, I believe
  which we have need to infuse into our colonies. Our kinfolk may be
  educated to this great ideal. Rome was not built in a day. A great
  empire on novel principles is not to be consolidated and
15 established in days, months or years; but we may be encouraged by
  the past to look to the future.

Joseph Chamberlain was not content to rely on rhetoric alone. He was determined to enact solid legislation and bring about real change. In the realm of imperial administration he advocated the idea of a federal structure similar to the relationship between the United States' central government and the individual states of the Union. The ultimate dream was a United States of Empire. The idea was that each colony would eventually have self-government over local affairs with defence and overall central government centred in an empire parliament in London. A federal system of government, with its emphasis on a strong central control while at the same time allowing for local government to legislate on matters of local concern, was something he greatly admired. The success of the United States system of federal government seemed to add strength to this argument.

The second policy he put forward was economic. He wanted to create a new customs union embracing the whole Empire. This would place a tariff on the goods of other nations. This idea was influenced by the success of the German customs union known as the *Zollverein*. The aim of the two policies taken together was to make the Empire a politically united and economically inter-dependent unit. This was an attractive idea in an age of economic, imperial, and military rivalry between the Great Powers. These dreams for the future were accompanied by a nightmare scenario. This argued that unless both policies were implemented the British Empire was in danger of collapse. To frighten the British voter Chamberlain constantly conjured up the picture of a British Empire

1 Face to face with great combinations, with enormous trusts, having behind them gigantic wealth. Even the industries and commerce which we thought peculiarly our own, even those are in danger. It is quite imposssible that these new methods of competition can be
5 met by adherance to old and antiquated methods which were perfectly right at the time at which they were developed. At the present moment the Empire is being attacked on all sides and, in our isolation, we must look to ourselves. We must draw closer our internal relations, the ties of sentiment, the ties of sympathy, yes,
10 and the ties of interest. If by adherance to economic pedantry, to old shibboleths, (e.g. free trade) we are to lose opportunities of closer union which are offered by our colonies if we are to put aside occassions now within our grasp, if we do not take every chance in our power to keep British trade in British hands, I am certain we
15 shall deserve the disasters which will infallibly come upon us. These days are for great Empires and not for little states.

As Colonial Secretary between 1895 and 1903 Joseph Chamberlain had a golden opportunity to attempt to create his United States of Empire with a clear protectionist economic policy.

As a first step toward greater unity Chamberlain invited representatives from all the colonies to a series of Colonial Conferences held in London. These provided him with an opportunity to put his ideas for imperial unity to the leaders of the Empire. At the 1897 Conference he proposed 'a great council for the Empire'. This received hardly any support. The idea of a Federal Imperial Parliament for the whole Empire was also rejected, as was the suggestion for a customs union for the Empire. The suggestion that the colonies should pay equal shares of the defence bill for the Empire was dismissed out of hand. These colonial conferences turned into 'talking shops' at which a great deal of food and drink was consumed, a great deal of hot air was generated, but no plan for the future of the Empire was ever agreed. Chamberlain was not able to enthuse the people who mattered with his vision. They felt that they had much to lose and little to gain from an Empire with strengthened central control.

Yet, although Chamberlain failed to make any headway with his 'grand design', he did manage to bring about a number of more limited reforms that had lasting significance. He encouraged Australia to develop a Federal Constitution - which exists to this day. He introduced schemes to improve health. Schools of Tropical Medicine were established in London and Liverpool and research into malaria and sleeping sickness - Africa's worst plagues at the time - produced important findings. He also set up an Agricultural Department in the West Indies to advise on the best use to make of land, and he gave government money to the islands to establish a steamer service to America and Britain and to stimulate trade.

However, Chamberlain's period at the Colonial Office was overshadowed by the part he played in events in South Africa which led up to the outbreak of the Boer War. This was a costly failure - as we shall see in chapter 6. In 1903, his period as Colonial Secretary ended in dramatic fashion. He resigned to form the ill-fated Tariff Reform League. This created as much controversy within the Conservative and Unionist Parties as did his colonial policy. The Tariff Reform League aimed to persuade the government to tax all non-Empire goods that entered Britain. The proceeds were to be used for social reform and the development of the Empire. The move split the Conservatives and Unionists, helped unite the Liberal Party, and was the prime reason the Conservatives lost the 1906 and 1910 general elections. Chamberlain himself had a stroke in 1906 and never again took a leading role in politics. By 1914 the Conservative Party had dropped Tariff Reform from its party programme, the Empire was not united, and the idea of an imperial *Zollverein* had been rejected by the electorate.

4 The Empire, Jingoism and the Working Class

The change from indifference to enthusiasm towards the Empire was not just confined to the major political leaders of the late-Victorian period. It was reflected throughout British society. Historians are agreed that the greatest enthusiasts for imperialism came from upper- and middle-class élite groups and from those who had some direct interest in the Empire. Support was particularly strong in upper-class public school élite groups such as the landed aristocracy, the officer class in the army and navy, colonial administrators, and among middle-class business-men. There was also support among rising middle-class groups such as shopkeepers and white collar workers, and among many members of the skilled sections of the working class. The imperialistic Boy Scout and

Girl Guide movements and the pro-Empire newspapers such as the *Daily Mail* and the *Daily Express* were most popular among these groups.

However, the extent of working-class support for imperialism has generated a large amount of controversy among historians. The most popular contemporary explanation of popular enthusiasm for the Empire was that put forward by J.A. Hobson in his famous work *Imperialism: A Study* (1902). Hobson was a Liberal and had been a war reporter during the Boer War. He put forward the view that the imperial crusade by the Conservative Party had won over the working classes in the late-Victorian age and he also believed the working classes had been manipulated into supporting the idea of imperial expansion by 'small groups of businessmen and politicians who know what they want and know how to get it'. He argued that the 'popular imperialism' that emerged after 1870 was:

1

A depraved choice of national life. It is only the competing cliques of businessmen that are forcing the Empire to the top of the political agenda. Imperialism is motivated not by the interests of
5 the nation but by those of certain classes who impose the policy of the nation for their own advantage. Imperialism also favours the general cause of Conservatism by diverting public interest and attention away from domestic agitation and the tension it causes in international relations encourages increased military expenditure
10 and provides a justification for not implementing social reform.

This view of small upper-class élites deliberately seeking to fill the 'empty heads' of an uncritical working class with propaganda was based on contemporary observations of working-class public demonstrations of support for the Empire and British military victories abroad. It quickly came to be accepted as the orthodox explanation of working-class support for imperialism. Yet Richard Price, in *An Imperial War and the Working Class* (1976), raised doubts about whether the working class was ever as pro-Empire as had been suggested. He wrote, 'the existence of an uncritical jingoistic working class from 1880 to 1906 has been so uncritically accepted that it has achieved the status of historical truth without ever being seriously examined'. In claiming this, Price was echoing the questioning of the evidence, upon which the case for widespread working-class enthusiasm for empire was based, that had recently been taking place. For example, Henry Pelling had raised doubts about the wisdom of using the wording of music hall songs as proof of working-class sentiments. In *Popular Politics in the Late Victorian Age* (1967) he had written, 'A song such as *Beer Glorious Beer* may be taken as evidence of the popularity of beer, but it does not indicate a rising consumption of beer in 1900 nor the proportion of heavy drinkers to teetotalers in the working class as a whole'. His contention was that the claim that the working class was jingoistic because certain songs were popular in the music halls remains unproven. The contemporary claim that the large numbers of working-class men who enlisted for the Boer War were jingoistic has also been attacked. Price claimed that poverty and unemployment, rather than patriotism or love of the Empire, were the primary reasons for enlistment. The revisionists also cast doubt on the popularly held view that outbursts of popular enthusiasm in working-class areas indicated support for imperialism. Pelling had claimed that there is a telling distinction to be made between the small number of times the working class danced in the streets in support of the Empire - such as on Disraeli's return from Berlin and on the night of the relief of Mafeking during the Boer War - and the more frequent participation of middle- and upper-class groups in public patriotic celebrations.

The revionists also attacked the view that the Conservative victory in the 1900 'Khaki Election' was yet another indicator of working-class support for the Empire. The Boer War was certainly the key issue in the election. Yet the Conservatives polled only 400,000 more votes (out of a total of 4.5 million) than the Liberal Party, which was divided over support for the war. Jingoistic candidates from the Conservative and Liberal parties were rejected in many working-class constituencies. It seems that, among the urban working classes in 1900, opposition to Irish Home Rule remained a stronger reason than imperialism for voting Conservative. Revisionists claim that whatever electoral benefits the Conservatives gained from imperialism soon evaporated. By 1902 they were losing by-elections and in 1906 the Liberals won a landslide victory. This defeat showed that the British public was not prepared to consolidate the Empire if it meant a lower standard of living.

Yet the revisionists' view that the predominant attitude of the working class towards imperialism was indifference has subsequently come under attack by a group of historians led by J.M. MacKenzie who have sought to show how much effort Conservative imperialists devoted to winning working-class support for the British Empire. This research indicates that imperial propaganda had a much greater impact on the working class than was previously indicated by revisionist historians. A good deal of oral history is also revealing that the excitement engendered by imperialism in the music hall, elections and popular literature had a marked impact on the working class. The idea that people who participated in jingoistic celebrations and rowdyism were mainly drawn from the so-called 'respectable classes of society' has been called into question in a number of studies.

5 The Empire and Popular Culture

The work of MacKenzie has stimulated a flood of studies looking at the impact of the Empire on popular culture. MacKenzie's own *Propaganda and Empire* (1984) has now become a classic of its kind, in which he shows how imperialists attempted to manipulate British public opinion in the fashion almost of a propaganda ministry. They pushed propaganda through school textbooks, in popular literature, and in the music hall.

This imperial propaganda laid great stress on the idea of British racial superiority. A typical example is the popular poem, *The White Man's Burden,* by Rudyard Kipling.

> Take up the White Man's Burden –
> Send forth the best ye breed –
> Go bind your sons to exile
> To serve your captives' need;
> To wait in heavy harness
> On fluttered folk and wild –
> Your new-caught, sullen peoples
> Half-devil and half-child.

The idea of 'Englishness' as a higher form of civilisation was also reflected in school textbooks, such as *The School History of England,* written by Kipling and Fletcher which suggested that

> the aim of every boy is to love his country more and more, to praise her sovereign dominion in every part of the globe to support Britain's brave soldiers in battle and thank God England made him such a happy child.

Sentiments of racial superiority were prominent in popular literature aimed at youth. The two most popular imperialist novelists of the day were Rider Haggard and G.A. Henty. Their stories glorified the use of force to achieve Britain's imperialist aims. The heroes of imperialist literature are always male, combine good looks, good breeding (usually aristocratic), and great physical strength. All the opponents to Britain fail because they lack these truly 'English qualities'. The British officer is portrayed as a superman leading the best troops or naval crew in all the world. The working class is always portrayed as 'loyal and honest as the day is long'. The message put across in the majority of imperialist literature is that Britain cannot lose in its imperialist adventures.

It has been shown by Penny Summerfield in *Imperialism and Popular Culture* (1986) that the Victorian and Edwardian music halls also had a strong imperialist emphasis. The music halls were an adult form of popular entertainment aimed primarily at the working classes. It seems there was a concerted effort by pro-Conservative imperialists to push jingoism at the working classes in the music halls, especially after 1900 when a spate of imperialist shows began to appear. The emphasis on the racial superiority of the English was a feature of many music hall songs, such as 'It's the English speaking race against the world'.

We're brothers of the self same race
speakers of the self same tongue
With the same brave hearts that feel no fears
from fighting for a thousand years
Folks say what will the British do?
Will she rest with banners furled?
No No No
When we go once again to meet the foe
It's the English speaking race against the world.

Two of the heroes of the music hall were Jolly Jack Tar, a popular sailor, and Tommy Atkins, an honest working-class bloke who joined the army. Not suprisingly, the two most popular songs of the imperialist era were 'All the Nice Girls Love a Sailor', and 'Tommy Atkins You're Alright'.

Tommy, Tommy, Tommy with your heart so big and warm
Don't he look a picture in his dandy uniform
To keep our flag a flying, he's a doing and a dying
Every single inch of him's a soldier and a man.

This research has found that the majority of these imperialist songs and pieces of popular literature on the imperial theme supported a very 'jingoistic' view of empire. But it is difficult to assess what impact this literature had on the people at whom it was aimed. There is no doubt that it did have some effect. The question is, how much? This is a difficult question to answer because quantifiable evidence does not exist. One approach historians have used is to collect oral evidence from people who lived through the times. From this it appears that large numbers of young people did grow up accepting many of the ideas they encountered in popular literature. The fascination with royalty, the armed forces, and racial superiority in the music hall songs of the day seems to have influenced many of those who were exposed to it. Many of those interviewed remembered being swept along at times by the patriotic fervour that surrounded them.

This new field of study has raised new questions about the impact of the Empire on the working class. A great deal of popular imperial propaganda glorified the idea of Britain being engaged in a civilising mission. It made war, the armed forces, and imperialist adventures focal points of popular entertainment and mass celebration. The working class was not completely immune from these forces nor was British society as a whole.

Making notes on *'The Empire, British Politics and Popular Culture in the Age of Imperialism'*

As the issues discussed in this chapter are less 'mainstream' than those featured in the rest of the book it is important that you think carefully about why you are doing it before you spend time making notes on what you have just read. In particular, you should have a clear idea about the use you expect to make of whatever notes you take. Certainly, there is little likelihood that a routine set of detailed notes on the whole chapter will be what you need. You will need to be selective.

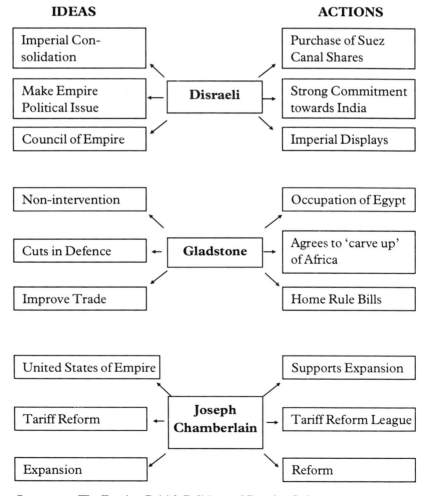

Summary - The Empire, British Politics and Popular Culture

Answering essay questions on 'The Empire, British Politics and Popular Culture in the Age of Imperialism'

Examiners' reports often point to three main weaknesses in candidates: a) failing to read the wording of questions carefully, b) making poor decisions about what material is relevant to a question, and, c) answering the question that it was hoped would be set rather than the one that actually was.

The type of question you would probably hope to find on an examination paper after reading this chapter might be:

1   Compare and contrast the policies of Gladstone and Disraeli towards the British Empire.

Study its wording carefully. It is a classic 'Compare and contrast' question and should be one of the standard types of question you are used to tackling by the time you reach the end of your course. The only potential snag seems to be for those who do not read questions carefully and who therefore will not realise that the task is to discuss *policies*, rather than all aspects of Gladstone and Disraeli's dealings with the Empire. Such a candidate is likely to exhibit the second of the common failings - selecting an amount of irrelevant material for inclusion. It would be a useful exercise to list the things about Gladstone and Disraeli which have appeared in this chapter but which would not be relevant to this question.

An example of the type of question you would not be pleased to encounter in an examination might be:

2   To what extent did Joseph Chamberlain attempt to practise what Disraeli had only preached about the Empire?

It is questions such as this which most often trap candidates into displaying the third of the common failings - answering the question they wanted rather than the one that has been set. This would normally take the form of writing almost exclusively about Joseph Chamberlain, with only a token mention of Disraeli. Such an approach would be a real recipe for disaster. What is needed is a methodical working through of essay-planning skills. The first two steps are the vital ones in this case. They should almost be second nature to you by the time you finish your course. They are: i) rephrase the question so as to clarify exactly what you are being asked to do, and, ii) identify any assumptions being made by the question which are in any sense controversial and which will therefore need to be discussed (normally in the introductory paragraph). It is the successful carrying out of the second step that will draw the sting of this particular question. What is the assumption about Disraeli that will need to be discussed? It always makes planning the rest of your answer much easier if you are able to conclude such discussions about assumptions made with a sentence such as, 'For the purposes of answering this question it will be best to act as if the assumption being made is correct'. Are there any circumstances in which it would be unwise to do this?

Source-based questions on 'The Empire, British Politics and Popular Culture in the Age of Imperialism'

1 Disraeli's Crystal Palace Speech (1872)
Carefully read the extract from the speech on pages 72-3. Answer the following questions.
a) Identify three major criticisms made of Liberal policy towards the Empire, using a brief quotation to illustrate each one. (6 marks)
b) Identify the two main suggestions made by Disraeli about future policy towards the Empire. (4 marks)
c) How far is it accurate to claim that 'Disraeli made no attempt to act on the basis of the Crystal Palace Speech in his dealings with the Empire during his period as Prime Minister'? (10 marks)

2 Joseph Chamberlain on the Empire
Carefully read the extract on page 80. Answer the following questions.
a) According to Chamberlain, in what ways is the Empire under attack? (3 marks)
b) What does Chamberlain consider the relationship between free trade and Empire to be? (3 marks)
c) Assess the usefulness of such a speech to a historian studying Chamberlain's imperial policy. (4 marks)

3 Joseph Chamberlain and the Future of the Empire
Carefully read the extract on page 79. Answer the following questions.
a) Using your own words, define 'the new concept of Empire' mentioned in the extract. (2 marks)
b) In what ways are Chamberlain's criticisms of past policy similar to the sentiments expressed by Disraeli in his Crystal Palace speech? (3 marks)
c) How far did Chamberlain attempt to put into practice the ideas outlined in the extract? Include quotes from the extract in your answer. (5 marks)

CHAPTER 6

The Crisis of Empire, 1895-1914: The Boer War and its Consequences

The climax of all the imperial excitement of the late-nineteenth century was reached during the Anglo-Boer War. A 'mighty' British imperial army (which at one stage numbered 450,000 men) faced a Boer army of less than 100,000 independent farmers, who lacked training, ammunition, supplies and long-range weapons. To defeat them the British army burned farms, crops, and villages, divided the countryside into zones with barbed wire fences, and captured soldiers, women and children and placed them in concentration camps. The war began in 1899 and ended in 1902. When it was all over 22,000 British lives had been lost, £250 million pounds had been spent, and over 20,000 South Africans had perished in the concentration camps. Britain had suffered international humiliation. 'Britain's Vietnam' is how one historian describes the South African War. The Boer War was a deeply significant event in the history of the Empire from 1815 to 1914, with far reaching consequences.

1 The Road to War, 1895-9

The immediate cause of the war revolved around an argument between Britain and the Transvaal over voting rights for European immigrants employed in gold and diamond mines in South Africa. The British government wanted the independent Boer republic to grant full citizenship rights to these 41,000 strong, mainly British, immigrant 'Uitlanders' (outsiders). Paul Kruger, the Transvaal President, believed the Uitlander issue was being used by the British government as a way of ending the independence of the Boer Republics. If the Uitlanders had been given full voting rights they would have eventually grown strong enough to elect a government of their own choosing. This was a prospect the fiercely independent Boers would not contemplate. Throughout the crisis, Kruger retained the conviction that the British government would not compromise over the issue.

The Uitlander dispute was really the final straw in a long-standing Anglo-Boer antagonism. In the late-seventeenth century the Dutch East India Company had set up a small trading station near the Cape of Good Hope on the southern tip of South Africa (Cape Colony). The poorest members of this deeply Protestant community were grazing farmers who called themselves *treboers* (also known as Boers) and searched for land, at the expense of Africans. The Boers viewed themselves as a distinct and unique group of pilgrims, called themselves 'Afrikanders' (the people of Africa), spoke a variant of Dutch they called 'Afrikaans', and were hostile to both Africans and Europeans.

In 1806 the British navy captured Cape Colony. Henceforth, the Cape of Good Hope became a crucial naval base for Britain on the trade route to India and the Far East. In 1834 the British abolished slavery. A group of 5,000 Boers refused to accept the decision, crossed the Orange and Vaal rivers on the 'great trek', and set up two independent states (Transvaal and the Orange Free State) These 'Boer Republics' enshrined their unique Protestant identity and language in their constitutions. The Boers were determined to exclude Africans (and anyone else) from voting in their elections.

By 1855 the British government had recognised the independence of these two countries. But this did not stop Anglo-Boer relations remaining tense. In 1877 Britain took control of the Transvaal (over the Zulu threat). In 1881 Paul Kruger (Transvaal President) attacked the British (First Boer War) because they refused to restore independence to the Boer Republic after the Zulu war. After a Boer victory over the British at Majuba Hill the British government decided to restore partial independence. This was done under two agreements signed in 1882 and 1884. But the treaties contained two provisos. Firstly, Britain supervised foreign policy, and secondly, the British retained the right to intervene, in certain circumstances, in domestic matters. The dispute between the Transvaal and the British government over the Uitlander issue revolved around the interpretation of the wording of the agreements that followed the first Anglo-Boer war.

In addition to the disagreement over the extent of British rights in the Transvaal, there was an underlying economic dimension to the dispute. In the late-nineteenth century gold and diamonds were discovered in Cape Colony and the Transvaal. This 'mineral revolution' transformed the economic balance in the region. The Transvaal suddenly changed from being a backward agricultural economy into a country which was rapidly increasing in prosperity and which threatened to dominate the British colonies in South Africa. However, much of the Transvaal's new wealth was in the hands of British and German gold and diamond mineowners ('Rand millionaires') who had established mines in the area, having attracted large amounts of British investment.

The economic role played by the 'Rand millionaires' in the origins of the war has been the subject of historical controvery ever since. It appears that the major mineowners did support the Uitlanders' claims for voting rights, primarily, it seems, because they believed that it would be difficult to attract British and European skilled workers to an area in which they were denied basic civil rights. The obstinacy that the Transvaal government showed towards the Uitlanders was viewed as a severe handicap in the continuing effort to attract labour and investment, both of which were vital for long-term expansion. Therefore, the 'Rand millionaires' felt that they stood to profit from an extension of voting rights to the Uitlanders. Indeed J.A. Hobson claimed that the war was caused by a 'conspiracy of financiers' for whom the Uitlander issue was a cloak to hide a desire for private profit. This view was supported by Thomas Pakenham in *The Boer War* (1979) who claimed that leading mineowners 'were active partners' with Lord Milner in the making of the war. This probably overstates the case. In his brilliant study, *The Origins of the South African War* (1983), Andrew Porter claimed that 'the British government was tightening the screws on the Transvaal from 1895', but he rejected the view that it was the puppet of the mining magnates. Cain and Hopkins added weight to this argument by asserting that the British government and the Colonial Office were leading the drive to place pressure on the Transvaal in support of broader strategic, political and economic aims which included (but was not dominated by) the desires of the mineowners.

The roles played by Joseph Chamberlain, the Colonial Secretary, and Sir Alfred Milner, British High Commissioner for South Africa, remain the most vital elements in explaining why Britain went to war. Both Chamberlain and Milner did express concerns about the dangers for British interests in Southern Africa of a vibrant and independent Transvaal seemingly determined to cause difficuties for British interests in the region.

For his part, Joseph Chamberlain soured Anglo-Boer relations in the run up to war in three ways. Firstly, he informed Kruger that the agreements Britain had signed at the end of the First Boer War had not -- as the Transvaal government believed - restored full control over domestic policy to the Republic. Secondly, he appointed Alfred Milner, a man who was known to be hostile to the Transvaal, as High Commissioner for South Africa. Thirdly, he succesfully encouraged the City of London to deny the Transvaal loans for long-term investment. Yet whether Chamberlain did all this as part of a deliberate plan to instigate a war with the Boer Republics remains open to question. It appears he wanted the Transvaal to accede to British demands on behalf of the Uitlanders, short of going to war. No convincing evidence has yet emerged to prove that he wanted war all along.

The leading candidate for 'warmonger' is Alfred Milner, the British High Commisioner for South Africa. Milner had his finger in every pie. He placed enormous pressure on the Transvaal government in the run up to the war. He constantly pressed the Uitlander issue, whipped up anti-Boer feeling in the South African and British press, put pressure on the City of London to deny the Transvaal capital, gained support from the 'Rand millionaires' and persuaded many leading figures in the Unionist government to support him. Milner was convinced there was a 'greater issue than the grievances of the Uitlanders at stake ... our supremacy in South Africa ... and our existence as a great power in the world is involved'.

Milner also personally conducted the negotiations with the Transvaal government. In all his dealings with Kruger he took an aggressive and uncompromising stance. He demanded that the Uitlanders be granted full citizenship of the Transvaal within five years. In May 1899 Kruger met him in a final attempt to settle the dispute. At the meeting Kruger offered the Uitlanders full citizenship within seven years in return for British recognition of the independence of the Transvaal in domestic matters, and he expressed a willingness to discuss all outstanding issues at an international conference in Europe. Milner rejected both offers point blank. Kruger's response that 'it is our country you want' would seem an accurate reflection of the situation.

It seems clear that 'Milner stirred the pot' and pushed everyone to the brink of war. Yet few historians are now prepared to suggest that he was deliberately planning to achieve his aims by war. It appears that Milner, and most of his supporters, believed Kruger would 'bluff up to the canon's mouth' and would then accept British demands. The failure of the Cabinet, Milner, the Colonial Office and War Office to make adequate preparation for an armed struggle certainly adds weight to this interpretation. It seems that the long-term economic growth of the Transvaal, which was likely to turn it into the major power in Southern Africa, led to a fundamental conflict of interests between Britain and the Republic. As Cain and Hopkins put it, 'Milner helped to stir the pot. He did not supply the ingredients. More important were the British government and, indirectly, the mine owners'.

By the autumn of 1899 Chamberlain, the Cabinet, the majority of MPs and the press had all swung around to Milner's earlier view that the Boers needed 'teaching a lesson'. British troops were sent to South Africa to exert the final pressure on Kruger. The Boers were now left with two choices. They could either accept British demands or they could fight for their independence. They chose the latter option. On 9 October 1899 Kruger sent a telegram demanding Britain remove its troops from the Transvaal border or he would declare war. At the same time he offered to settle the matter at an international conference. The British government did not even reply. On 11 October the Transvaal (much to the surprise of Milner) launched the attack on Cape Colony which started the Boer War. On hearing this news Lord Salisbury, the British Prime Minister, said, 'this has relieved us of the task of explaining to the British public why we are at war'. The full weight of the 'mighty' British Empire was now ranged against a mainly farming community. The general view in Britain was that 'it will all be over by Christmas'.

There remains one question to be answered in examining the causes of the war. Why did Kruger decide to fight? It appears that he never believed that the British were bluffing. He was absolutely convinced (especially after the Jameson Raid) that the British wanted to end the independence of the Transvaal. Once this seemed clear, Kruger was determined that the Boers would fight. The Transvaal government never did want to concede voting rights to the Uitlanders. In the 1890s arms had been purchased from Germany in preparation for a war which Kruger and most of his supporters saw as 'inevitable'. Kruger's resolve was stiffened by the leading Boer generals (especially Smuts) who constantly advised the President that if war came the British could be defeated. Kruger also knew that he could rely completely on Boer farmers to fight bravely to preserve their indepenence. A large number of Boers did believe a war with Britain might end up with the same result as the American War of Independence - a United States of Southern Africa under the leadership of the Transvaal. It seems that the Transvaal was more determined (and better prepared) to fight than Milner had anticipated.

2 The Course of the War, 1899-1902

In the early months of the war Britain suffered a series of humiliating defeats at the hands of the Boers who laid siege to the towns of Ladysmith, Kimberly and Mafeking. In one 'black week' in December 1899 the British lost battles at Stromberg, Magersfontein and Colonso. In January 1900 a further British defeat occurred at Spion Kop.

These early setbacks shook British confidence. They were the result of poor planning by the War Office and poor leadership by the generals. The British underestimated the Boers and had failed to ensure that adequate troops and essential supplies of food and ammunition were in place ready for the conflict. The solution was to send more troops, to improve supply lines, and to dispatch Lord Roberts ('hero of the Indian Mutiny') and Lord Kitchener ('hero of the Sudan') to take command of the British war effort.

This was the real military turning point in the war. Kitchener and Roberts re-organised the supply situation and developed a clear strategy to defeat the Boers. The towns of Kimberly, Ladysmith and Mafeking, the latter town had held out for 217 days, were all relieved in quick succession, producing scenes of jubilation never before seen on the streets of Britain. By June 1900 British forces were moving swiftly towards complete victory. Johannesburg and Pretoria, the capital of the Transvaal, were occupied. Paul Kruger and his government took flight to Europe (Kruger died in exile in 1904).

In the summer of 1900 Britain basked in the glory of its seemingly swift and overwhelming victory over the 'bloody Boers', as they were termed in the popular press. Kitchener and Roberts returned to Britain sure that the war was as good as over. In October 1900 the Unionist government cashed in on the war euphoria by staging the famous 'Khaki Election' and were rewarded with victory over the Liberal Party. Yet these celebrations were premature. The Boer armies had not given up. In fact, they refused to surrender and headed for the countryside to fight one of the most gritty guerilla campaigns ever waged by a small power against a major world power until the Vietnam War of the 1960s and 1970s.

In 1901 the Boers invaded Cape Colony. Lord Kitchener returned once more to South Africa. He was absolutely determined to deal 'once and for all' with the guerilla tactics of the enemy. The tactics he used were a political blunder and caused enormous controversy. He divided the country into zones and sectioned them off with barbed wire. The idea was to impede the movement of Boer soldiers. In order to prevent the Boer soldiers from replenishing their stocks of food Kitchener introduced a 'scorched earth policy'. This consisted of burning Boer villages, destroying crops, capturing cattle, and collecting the civilian population in something called 'concentration camps'.

3 The Home Front: Radicals against the Boer War

The conditions in these concentration camps created an international outcry and in Britain produced an influential body of organised criticism against the war. This was led by radicals in the Liberal Party, the Labour Party, and among socialists. Henry Campbell-Bannerman, the Liberal leader, summed up the general feeling of the opponents of war in a speech in 1901.

1 A phrase is often used that war is war in relation to the conditions
  in the camps. But, when one asks what is going on in South Africa
  the government says there is no war, it is a local dispute. So I ask
  when is a war not a war? When it is carried on with the methods of
5 barbarism now used in South Africa.

This 'methods of barbarism' view dominated the arguments of the organised opponents of the war - the pro-Boers. Many of the opponents took a religious and humanitarian tone. It was Liberal radicals who led the attacks against the war even though the pro-Boers failed to persuade the Liberal Party leadership to back their cause. The Liberal Opposition saw it as their constitutional duty to express loyalty to the policy of the government in time of war. In fact, a large number of leading Liberals - Grey, Haldane, Asquith and Rosebery - were 'Liberal imperialists' who supported the war. The radicals, among whom Lloyd George was numbered, only made up about a third of Liberal MPs.

The pro-Boers concentrated their attacks on the 'jingoistic' Unionist government. They sent the radical Emily Hobhouse to South Africa to produce a report on the conditions in the concentration camps. She revealed that they were surrounded by barbed wire, that 12 prisoners shared a small bell tent, that there was no soap, no toilets, no mattresses, and few blankets, and that rations were below starvation level. She concluded that 'the army have no humanity' and that many soldiers admitted the war was a 'gigantic mistake'. The pro-Boers later sent Joshua Rowntree, a renowned expert on poverty, to report on conditions, but he was refused entry into the camps.

The growing left-wing socialist press went even further in its denunciation of the war, which they argued was being fought by a 'privileged few' for 'capitalist aims'. Here are three typical examples of the views put forward by the socialist press;

a) The war is fought for greedy ghouls who rejoice in the fact that every drop of blood will eventually be turned into gold for themselves.

b) The stock exchange gang have engineered this war so that Britain shall destroy the independence of the Boer Republics and save Rhodesia from bankruptcy.

c) Joseph Chamberlain dragged Britain into this nice little war which is run by an unscrupulous minister [Chamberlain] and an unscrupulous propagandist [Milner].

However, it is clear that the views of the radicals and the socialist press did not reflect a broader public opposition to the war among the working class and in Britain as a whole. H.F. Wyatt, who spoke at numerous anti-Boer War meetings, recorded that there was a 'violent selfishness in the working class areas I visited'. But Wyatt found few working-class people who believed the war was being fought - as the government claimed - to obtain democratic rights for the Uitlanders.

Joseph Chamberlain and Lord Kitchener 'sending the Innocents to Heaven'. This cartoon appeared in a German magazine Ulk *(1901)*

Even working-class soldiers were sceptical about this. One typical letter from a soldier recorded, 'I don't see the point of it. We are all half starved all the time. It's the worst war ever and all for gold mines'.

The world-wide outrage against the concentration camps was much more pronounced. The war received enormous coverage in the German press. The German Chancellor, Von Bulow, denounced British treatment of Boer prisoners as 'brutal and inhuman.' German newspapers and magazines produced hostile cartoons (see page 95). The general international view of Britain was of 'a bully of women and children, and a very inefficient one at that'. The supposed 'defender of the weak' was in fact doing just the opposite.

At first, the British government refused to accept the claims made about the 'barbaric' concentration camps. It claimed that the camps were 'voluntary' and refused to give details about the number of people who had died in them. To this day no exact figures exist. Numbers as low as 20,000 and as high as 28,000 have been claimed. In 1901 the British government did finally give in to radical pressure for an enquiry. A commission led by Millicent Fawcett, a leading member of the women's suffrage movement, visited the camps and recommended several improvements including more nurses and improved rations. As a result, conditions did improve. Yet the whole affair had been deeply damaging.

4 Peace

Meanwhile, in South Africa the war dragged on. It required 450,000 troops recruited from all over the Empire finally to defeat the Boers. In May 1902 the Boer leaders surrendered at Vereeniging. It had taken over two years for the mighty British Empire to humble a relatively small number of independent-minded farmers. The British lost 22,000 soldiers, 25,000 Boers died and approximately 12,000 Africans were killed. The war had been costly in money as well as lives. As Lloyd George said, 'every shell fired amounted to the cost of a pension for an old person in Britain'.

The peace terms the Boers were offered reflected the general view that the war had been a major blunder. All Afrikaaner prisoners who signed an oath of loyalty to the British crown were freed from the concentration camps. The damage to the Boer farms and villages was enormous. Over 400,000 horses, mules and donkeys perished. As part of the peace settlement, the British agreed to pay the costs of war damage. A total of 63,000 claims were received from Boer farmers. The British also offered loans for re-building, promised to safeguard the Afrikaaner language in any future constitution, and pledged to restore free elections and self-government at the earliest opportunity.

The poet Rudyard Kilping - a strong supporter of imperialism - summed up the public mood in Britain towards the war.

Let us admit it fairly as a business people should
We had no end of a lesson.
It will do us no end of good.

5 The Consequences of the Boer War

a) The Damage to the Unionist Government

The Unionist government which led Britain into the war was damaged
by its consequences. Alfred Milner refused to accept the responsibility
for what had gone wrong. He put all the blame on the poor planning for
war by the government. By 1902 he was writing, 'Why keep an Empire
for people who are dead set on chucking it away?'. In 1904 he agreed to
demands from the 'Rand' magnates to import Chinese labourers to
work in the South African gold mines. This confirmed the radical view
that 'the war was fought for the profits of the gold mines'- not the
interests of the Uitlanders. When it became known that the Chinese
were being flogged for insubordination by the mineowners an outcry
followed which led to a vote of censure being tabled against Milner in
the House of Commons. The press voiced bitter criticism. The 'Chinese
slavery' issue formed a leading part of the Liberal campaign in the 1906
election, but by then Milner had already been recalled by the Liberal
government which had taken office in the previous year.

b) The Growth of Anti-Imperialism

The war also led to a definite anti-imperialist group emerging within
British politics and society. Before the war the worst motive attributed to
supporters of imperialism was excessive patriotism. Imperialism could
even be seen as a 'positive mission' designed to bring 'civilisation' to
underdeveloped societies. It attracted supporters from all the major
political parties. After the war this was no longer the case. Imperialism
became synonomous with 'maverick politicians', 'capitalist cliques', and
'methods of barbarism'. As such it became seen as a right-wing policy
associated with 'die-hard' Conservatives.

Richard Koebner in 'The Meaning of Imperialism' *(Economic History
Review*, 1949) showed how the very meaning of the word imperialism
changed from a positive one before the Boer War to a negative one
afterwards. J.A. Hobson in his very influential study *Imperialism* (1902)
produced a coherent and successful attack on imperialism. Hobson
argued that by their actions in the Boer War the imperialists 'had
jeopardised the entire wealth of the nation in rousing strong resentment
of other nations for no real gain'.

c) The 'Revolution' in British Foreign Policy

The war also brought about a 'a revolution in British foreign relations'. Before the Boer War Britain believed itself strong enough to follow an independent foreign policy. This was popularly known as 'splendid isolation', the most important feature of which was that no military alliances were entered into with other major powers. However, the difficulties experienced during the protracted conflict revealed that the policy was no longer tenable. Soon after the war the policy was abandoned. Britain sought diplomatic agreements with imperial rivals anywhere she could find them. The Anglo-Japanese Alliance (1902), the Anglo-French Entente (1904), and the Anglo-Russian Convention (1907) followed in rapid succession. In addition, differences with the USA over Venezuela were settled and American domination of the North American continent was accepted.

d) The Growth of Anglo-German Antagonism

The war also contributed to the further souring of Anglo-German relations. In 1899 a number of leading members of the Unionist government had been in favour of an Anglo-German agreement. However, the frequent slanging matches which took place between the British and German press and between British and German politicians over the concentration camp scandal made it unlikely that there would be an Anglo-German 'understanding'.

Anglo-German antagonism intensified between 1902 and 1914. Many of the leading British imperialists who had supported the war switched their attention away from problems in Africa and towards those in Europe. It was widely believed that the Boer War had revealed what was described as the 'weakening of the British race'. As a result, imperialists tended to become 'scaremongers', forming themselves into a whole range of military and naval pressure groups, such as the National Service League and the Imperial Maritime League. The Conservative press and periodicals, such as *A Nation at Arms* and *The National Review*, warned of German spies and of possible German invasions. Rifle and military clubs were formed. Baden-Powell, (later Lord Baden Powell), the 'hero of Mafeking', established the Boy Scout and the Girl Guide movements to instil military ideals in children. The emphasis in imperialist literature switched from 'bloody Boers' to a 'wild Kaiser'. The imperialist 'radical right' continued their troublemaking right up to the outbreak of war in 1914. But the focus of their agitation was on the dangers of Germany, Socialism, David Lloyd George, and Home Rule for Ireland. The previous emphasis on 'imperial expansion' was downplayed.

e) The Defence Review of the Edwardian Era

The war led to a major review of British defence. There were full-scale government investigations into military planning, the military needs of the Empire, recruitment, army and navy organisation, food and ammunition supply, and home defence. Even the poor health of working-class recruits (via the Physical Deterioration Committtee) for the Boer War was investigated. Army, navy and social reforms soon followed. Free School meals and medical examinations in schools were introduced after 1906. The Haldane Reforms of the Army (1907) led to the creation of a fully equipped British Expeditionary Force (BEF). This was designed to move quickly from Britain into battle overseas. A Territorial Army (TA) of voluntary part-time soldiers designed to protect Britain from invasion was also set up. The Fisher Reforms of the Navy in 1904 led to a greater concentration of naval power in Europe and to the creation of a new fleet of 'unsinkable' battleships known as 'Dreadnoughts'. The Germans responded by building their own versions, and for the first time British naval supremacy was threatened.

f) The End of the *Pax Britanica*

The war also damaged the widely held view that the British Empire spread peace and prosperity around the world. The idea that Britain was the 'world's policeman' who could be called upon in an emergency to defend the 'weak' nations against the ambitions of the strong was deeply discredited. The charge of police brutality was laid against the 'world's policeman'. The high moral tone Britain had struck in its diplomatic relations since the mid-nineteenth century rang hollow after the concentration camps of the Boer War. No longer was Britain in a position to give moral lectures to anybody.

g) The Legacy for South African Politics

In the years after the war what can now be seen as a potentially catastrophic political situation was allowed to develop in South Africa. In 1906 the Liberal government restored self-government and free elections (for white people) to the defeated states. In the 1907 elections the Afrikaaner Het Volk Party, which was committed to a Union of South Africa and racial segregation, won a sweeping victory with the support of the newly enfranchised Uitlanders. In 1910 the Orange River Colony, the Transvaal, and Cape Colony agreed to form the Union of South Africa. Louis Botha, one of the leading guerilla leaders who had defied the British during the Boer War, became its first Prime Minister. This Boer-dominated Union, because it was accorded complete self-government, was able to develop a racist state over which Britain

HAIL, KITCHENER!   VICTOR AND PEACEMAKER!

Lord Kitchener returns victorious from the Boer War as 'Victor and Peacemaker', Punch *cartoon, 9 July 1902*

was subsequently able to exercise no control.

h) The Move Towards Dominion Status

The other self-governing colonies (Australia, Canada and New Zealand) also sought a re-definition of their constitutional relationship with Britain in the years following the conflict. They objected to being called 'colonies'. The term implied they were still under the 'control' of Britain. In 1907 the word 'dominion' was used to describe all the self-governing areas of the Empire. An imperial Conference based on the principle 'one government, one vote' was set up to decide future constitutional disputes within the Empire. This meant that the 'dominions' could now outvote Britain on matters related to their own constitutional relationship with the mother country. This was independence in all but name.

6 Assessment: The Boer War as Catalyst?

The Boer War was clearly one of those rare turning points in the history of the Empire between 1815 and 1914. It cast a giant shadow over British attitudes towards the Empire and imperial defence in the period from 1902 to the outbreak of the First World War in 1914. Many contemporaries viewed it as 'the first nail in the coffin of the British Empire'. The historian Zara Steiner believes the Boer war was 'a catalyst' for a number of changes that were going on in the way Britain looked at itself, its Empire and its relations with the world. There are, of course, some historians who would dispute this. C.C. Eldridge, for example, has argued that the British Empire not only survived all the traumas produced by the Boer War but expanded as a result of its victory and became even more important for British trade and investment than it had ever been before. The economic statistics seem to support this interpretation. Between 1903 and 1914 British exports to the Empire increased by 32 per cent, imports from the Empire increased by 31 per cent, British trade with Africa doubled, and 42 per cent of all British overseas investment went to the Empire.

But, of course, the true impact of the Boer war cannot be measured in purely economic terms. Robert Blake has recently described the war as 'Britain's Vietnam'. This comparison is attractive. The difficulty America found in defeating the guerrilla tactics of the Vietcong has similarities with the obstacles Britain faced in overcoming the roaming bands of Boer cavalrymen. The bombing of Cambodia, the dropping of napalm, and the burning of Vietnamese villages all damaged America's reputation at home and abroad in the 1960s and early 1970s. As Vietnam marks the end of America's incredible self-confidence as a nation on the world stage in the post-1945 period, so we can see the

Boer War as having a similar psychological impact on Britain and its image in the world in the years leading to the First World War.

The Boer War really marks the dividing line between the passionate imperialism of late-Victorian England and the loss of self-confidence in Britain about its future that has typified the twentieth century. This loss of confidence may not have been completely warranted. But it was widely felt all the same. The war was the last time that a small colonial war aroused the passions of the British people until the the Falklands campaign in 1982.

After the Boer War the British never believed as strongly as they had before it that the British Empire was one on which the sun would never set. There were many who expressed pessimism about the future. In 1914 the Liberal Colonial Secretary expressed his belief that 'the Empire is held together by a silken cord: twist this cord into a whiplash and a crack of the lash would be the death knell of the Empire'. This shows how much the bungled attempt to teach the Boers a lesson had permeated the British view of its long-term relations with the people of its Empire.

Making notes on *'The Crisis of the Empire, 1895-1914: The Boer War and its Consequences'*

This chapter lays particular stress on the causes and the consequences of

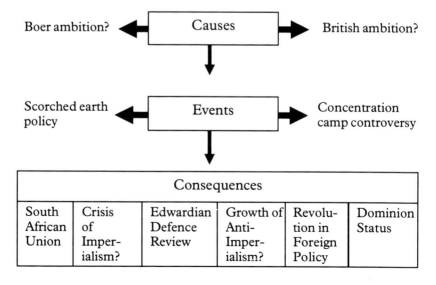

Summary - The Crisis of Empire, 1895-1914: The Boer War and its Consequences

the Boer War. A brief account of the course of the war is also included. It would therefore seem to be a good idea to compile your notes under three headings.

1 Causes. Draw up a list of the causes of the war. The roles of Kruger, Milner and Joseph Chamberlain are all important. It would also be worth including mention of the activities of Cecil Rhodes. Indicate the relative importance of each cause you explain.

2 Course. Divide the war up into its various stages, explaining the identifying features of each one. List the reasons why the war lasted for so long.

3 Consequences. Decide on the relative importance of the consequences. Note them in a descending order of importance.

Answering essay questions on '*The Crisis of the Empire, 1895-1914: The Boer War and its Consequences*'

Essay questions on the Boer War normally focus on the causes or the consequences, or both. It is very unlikely that you will be asked to give a chronological narrative of the fighting. The following are typical of the questions set on the Boer War.

1 What were the major consequences of the Boer War for Britain?

2 Explain the causes and the consequences of the Anglo-Boer War.

3 How far can Britain's part in causing the Boer War be justified?

4 Comment on the view that 'the Boer War was a blessing in disguise for Britain'.

Questions 1 and 2 are phrased just about as straightforwardly as is possible. The problem with such seemingly 'easy' questions is that every candidate who answers them is likely to produce a 'standard' answer, making it difficult for the examiner to do otherwise than to award a set of similarly mediocre marks. The skill in answering simple questions is to find an approach that allows your essay to stand out in some distinctive way. There are many ways of doing this. The approach that involves least risk of getting into a tangle is to answer the question from different points of view. In these cases the points of view could be those of contemporaries and of later commentators, or of Boers and British. What other points of view could be used to form the structure of an answer?

Questions 3 and 4 are much more challenging, and potentially much more rewarding. Both need to be 'unpacked' in the normal way. Question 3, in particular, opens up very easily once thought has been given to identifying just what is being asked of the candidate. In fact, two questions have been rolled into one. What are they? The second of the questions is about 'justification'. This means making judgements, which, of course, all has to do with criteria. What criteria would be appropriate to use in making judgements of Britain's actions during the lead-up to the Boer War? Once this has been decided the planning of an answer to question 3 should be fairly routine. Question 4 is full of fascinating possibilities. There are numerous acceptable ways in which it could be tackled. Any of them could yield a very good mark as long as some sense of balance is retained. The 'yes' and 'no' points do not need to be given exactly the same amount of space, but it would be dangerous to allow them to be too unequal - say outside the range of a 70:30 split.

Source-based questions on *The Crisis of Empire, 1895-1914: The Boer War and its Consequences'*

1 British and German Cartoonists' Views of the Boer War
Study carefully the two cartoons on pages 95 and 100. Answer the following questions.
a)   Comment on the way in which Kitchener and Chamberlain are portrayed in the *Punch* cartoon. (6 marks)
b)   What are the strengths and weaknesses of this cartoon as a historical source? (5 marks)
c)   Compare and contrast the presentation of British imperialism in the two cartoons. (9 marks)

CHAPTER 7

Conclusion

As we have seen throughout this book there were a whole host of social, economic and political reforms, treaties, wars, scrambles, riots and rebellions in the history of the British Empire between 1815 and 1914, about which historians can find little agreement. Despite all the efforts of Joseph Chamberlain, and his imperial supporters in the late-Victorian age, the Empire never became a uniform association in terms of its customs, language, religion, constitution, policy or law. It remained in 1914 what it had been in 1815: a visible expression of British power on the world stage.

One broad question historians have attempted to answer in relation to the British Empire in this period is, 'Whose interests was British imperialism serving?'. There have been many answers. The British claimed to be on a mission to 'bring the benefits of civilisation' to what they called 'the backward peoples of the world'. Cecil Rhodes claimed British imperialism was 'philanthropy plus 5 per cent'. In 1902 Hobson claimed that it served the interests of 'finance capitalists'. In 1916 Lenin felt that it served the interests of 'monopoly capitalists'. In 1919 Schumpeter claimed that late-Victorian imperialism was the last desperate throw of a 'dying aristocracy'. More recently, in 1993, Cain and Hopkins have suggested that it served the needs of 'gentlemanly capitalists' in the City of London.

Of course, the idea that the British Empire served narrow private interests has a very long history. The Americans fought the War of Independence in the eighteenth century on just such an assumption. And Adam Smith, the influential *laissez-faire* economist, in *The Wealth of Nations* (1776), argued that the colonies imposed heavy burdens on the British taxpayer, increased the threat of costly wars, and (most significantly) were run for the benefit of private commercial interests who were supported by 'corrupt' politicians.

The aim of this concluding chapter is to go beyond a mere summary of the previous chapters and to explore the important issue of whose interests the British Empire was serving in 1914. This is not a straightforward question to answer. In particular, it is not clear what criteria should be used in judging the costs and the benefits of an empire. Political? Social? Economic? Moral? Cultural? The list is potentially endless.

In recent decades the attention of historians has focused on the economic motives for British imperialism. An important study by two American scholars, Davis and Huttenback, *Mammon and the Pursuit of Empire: The Political Economy of British Imperialism, 1860-1912* (1986) explored the costs and benefits of the Empire and concluded that it was a waste of money for nearly all the British people except a select élite of peers, individual private companies and investors. This conclusion mirrored the mid-Victorian views of free traders who saw Empire as essentially costly and wasteful. The originality of Davis and Huttenback's work was the way in which the two writers approached the subject. A large team of research assistants explored a vast range of sources on business interests which were analysed using the latest state-of-the-art computer technonology. Other historians have criticised this approach on three counts. It has been argued that Davis and Huttenback examined only a randomly selected sample of British business interests; that they ignored the impact of imperial trade on the British economy; and that they paid little attention to the non-economic factors which often provide the explanation of why the British government and people supported imperialism. Nevertheless, a number of respected imperial historians, including Andrew Porter and Patrick O'Brien, believe that the two scholars have contributed significantly to historical study by opening up new ways of attempting to answer the question of whose interests British imperialism served. Economic questions are currently at the forefront of the present historical debate on British imperialism.

In the sections which follow an attempt will be made to identify the major costs and benefits of each of the main 'agents' involved in British imperialism in 1914.

1 The British Government

The main responsibilities the British government exercised towards the Empire were in the fields of administration and defence. One myth must be dispelled immediately. The administration of the British Empire was not an expensive, inefficient, giant, bureaucratic, 'jobs for the boys' jamboree for the declining British aristocracy. In fact, in 1914 fewer than 6,000 people were employed to administer the whole of the Empire. As India accounted for about 3,000 of these, this left less than 2,800 people to administer the rest! All Colonial administrators sat highly competitive examinations - they were not appointed merely because of who they knew. Of course, this fact might give a misleading impression as the nature of the exams and the class structure of the Victorian era meant that nearly all those who 'ran the Empire' came from affluent middle-class backgrounds, had been educated at public schools, and had attended Oxford or Cambridge Universities. Those outside this élite stood no chance of being appointed. This imperial administration, despite its seemingly privileged composition, was run very cheaply. The best estimate of the cost per head of the British people is about 20p a year.

However, the major cost of empire for the British government was not administration. It was defence. The cost of imperial defence grew rapidly between 1870 and 1914. New imperial rivals, the wars of the partition of Africa, border disputes in India, and the protection of trading interests in the Far East all added to the defence bill. The findings of recent research into the military expenditure of the major powers in the late-Victorian period shows that British defence expenditure was twice as high as that of Germany and France and roughly three times as high as that of Austria-Hungary, Russia, and the USA. The main item of defence expenditure was the Royal Navy. The other major expense was the Indian Army (340,000 troops).

Who paid the bill? It appears that British taxpapers footed the majority of it. The Indian people contributed nearly 70 per cent of the cost of the Indian army but nothing towards the cost of the navy. In 1912 the people of India contributed roughly 7p each towards the cost of their defence. By contrast, the colonies of settlement got off lightly. They paid only about 3p per person. This compares very well with the £1.56 paid per head by the British people for national defence, although it has been estimated that only about 54p of this sum could be said to have gone directly towards defending the Empire. The main reason for the increase in defence expenditure between 1903 and 1914 was the Anglo-German naval race - not imperial defence. Moreover, Paul Kennedy in *The Rise and Fall of the Great Powers* (1988) has shown that the majority of increased defence expenditure from 1900 to 1914 was financed by loans raised in the City of London which were added to the national debt. Therefore the real effects of increased defence expenditure were felt most acutely after 1914 when the earlier loans had to be paid back. Yet imperial defence did provide benefits for Britain. Virtually all the equipment for the Indian army was manufactured in Britain. Naval spending boosted British shipbuilding yards, which had full order books in 1914, employed nearly a million people, and made large profits for their owners. Another important benefit of the Empire was provided during the First World War. Canadian wheat helped to save Britain from starvation in 1917, a million troops drawn from all parts of the Empire fought bravely to hold the Germans at bay on the western front, and Canada provided the British war effort with vital supplies of ammunition.

2 Private Interests in Britain

The findings of recent historical research into industrial, financial and commercial interests have produced a complex cost-benefit picture.

a) British Industry

It is true to say that many companies made large profits from the Empire. The cotton industry of Lancashire is a prime example. One indication of this is that between 1850 and 1914 there were 15 new

Lancashire cotton-millionaires. Similar fortunes were made by various sugar, gold, iron, diamond, railway, steel, soap, biscuit, and timber companies. But it should be remembered that by no means all of the British companies that made large profits had any connection with the Empire. In fact, the majority of industrial wealth arose from trade outside the Empire. The major areas of British export growth between 1815 and 1875 were Europe, the USA, and Latin America, particularly Argentina - not the Empire. The Empire only became really important for British industrial export growth during the period 1870 to 1914. In 1875, 26 per cent of total exports went to the Empire. By 1914 this figure had risen to 35 per cent.

The primary reason the Empire became more important for industrial exports in the latter years of the nineteenth century was because British industry found it more difficult to sell goods to Germany, the USA and in eastern Europe. Between 1870 and 1900 the percentage of British exports going to the USA and Germany declined from 41 per cent to 30 per cent. As British industry found it more difficult to hold its own with its major competitors in their home markets, the Empire provided a relatively safe haven for British goods. Yet because British exporters had to compete on equal terms with foreign traders the British share of total trade with the Empire actually declined from 49 per cent in 1860 to 36 per cent in 1929. It is worth adding that British industrial exports declined even faster outside the Empire. British trade with the Empire became much more important for the British economy after the First World War than it had ever been before.

A number of historians have recently attempted to calculate what would have happened if Britain had abandoned the Empire in the nineteenth century and continued with protectionism rather than adopting free trade. Of course, this approach, known as the 'counter-factual approach', is highly speculative. Nevertheless, M. Edelstein in *The Economic History of Britain since 1700* (1981) has calculated that if Britain had abandoned the Empire after 1850 the loss of trade would have amounted to less than 3 per cent of the total and that the savings made on defence would have more than made up for this. In addition, he argued that the loss of the Empire in the mid-nineteenth century might have encouraged many British industries to diversify into new products and to modernise their plant and machinery to meet foreign competition. There is much about this hypothesis which makes sense. After 1914 many companies which relied exclusively on defence and the Empire as a 'captive market' did suffer a relative decline. Of course, this might just have been a result of the unimaginative management style of British industry, and possibly would have happened even had the Empire not existed.

b) The City of London

A great deal of recent research has centred on the role of the City of London - banks, finance houses, insurance companies, shipping interests and so forth. There is no doubt that huge profits were made by many 'finance capitalists' in the City of London from British imperialism. There were 22 new millionaires in merchant banking alone between 1860 and 1919. Yet only a quarter of the estimated £6 billion pounds invested abroad by the City after 1850 went to the Empire. There can be no suggestion that the City of London and 'finance capitalists' ever made investment decisions on patriotic grounds. They went in search for the best possible returns on their capital. These were often to be found outside the Empire, as the following table indicates.

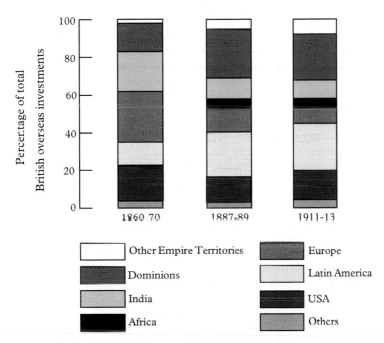

The Distribution of British Overseas Investment, 1860-1913

Nevertheless, in certain areas, where Britain moved towards formal involvement during the Partition of Africa, such as Egypt and South Africa, the role of financial investment cannot be ignored. Finance was certainly an important influence on the move towards British rule in both areas even though this was not the only reason. It also appears that banks and financial institutions did exert some pressure on the British government to act in their interests in some circumstances. For example, in Egypt, West Africa and East Africa this was certainly the case. On the other hand, the general proposition that investment by 'finance capitalists' was totally responsible for the drive towards the expansion of the Empire in the late-Victorian age is clearly impossible to sustain.

The best 'guesstimates' (as all figures on overseas investment are shaky) about returns on colonial investment suggest that they were highest in financial trusts, gold and diamond mining, construction projects (especially railways), and extractive industries. It is possible to find instances of individual investments in the Empire paying high dividends. But this proves very little. There were many investments in independent countries, especially in the USA and Latin America, which also made huge profits. Equally many colonial investments produced heavy losses. The East Africa Company went bust. The British South Africa Company paid no dividend between 1889 and 1923. Investment in tropical colonies in Africa was never very profitable.

Despite all the heated discussion of this question, historians have found it an impossible task to calculate an accurate balance sheet of all British investment in the Empire and to compare it with returns on investment elsewhere. One 'guesstimate' indicates that about two-thirds of British investment within the Empire went to the colonies of settlement and that the dependencies received about only one in every ten pounds lent overseas by British investors.

One surprising finding of recent research has been that profits from investment in the Empire between 1815 and 1870 - the so-called 'age of indifference' - were actually higher than from domestic stocks and shares. And, equally surprising, that profits from imperial investment between 1870 and 1914 - the so-called 'age of finance imperialism' - were actually lower than profits from investments in domestic stocks and shares. In other words, investing in the Empire before 1870 was relatively more profitable than it was between 1870 and 1914, the era when imperial investment has traditionally been thought to be an almost certain route to high profits.

On the equally vexed question of the relationship between government and business in the process of the 'new imperialism' no simple answers are possible. This is because the evidence does not exist which would allow researchers to establish whether British involvement in the 'new imperialism' was really a 'shady conspiracy' between 'gentlemanly capitalists' in the City of London and imperialists in the British government. By their very nature conspiracy theories are impossible to prove unless the conspirators come out into the open or leave traces of their activities behind them. The sources we can consult, including the private papers of the leading figures in the government and the Colonial Office from 1870 to 1914, show that the decisions to become directly involved in regions of Africa and Asia were never taken purely in the interests of industry or financiers in the City of London.

The British government considered economic, strategic, political, and what they saw as 'national' interests before taking action. The 'irrational' also came into play, as with the wild dreams of Rhodes and the grand plans of Chamberlain and Milner.

Perhaps the answer to this whole problem does, as has been suggested, lie in the 'unwritten' and 'unspoken' assumptions which were shared by the decision-makers in both the political and the financial worlds. In addition, the traditional history of the Empire may be 'what they wanted us to know'. The story of the dark corners - what happened 'behind closed doors'- of the government-business relationship over British imperialism in the period 1815 to 1914 is fascinating but tantalisingly elusive. The evidence to show exactly how the financiers 'pulled the strings' does not exist. As a result, any theory of government-business collaboration in British imperialism between 1815 and 1914 will always remain highly subjective and speculative.

c) The British People

Attempting to draw up a gains and losses balance sheet for the different classes in Britain is even more difficult. Not surprisingly, most research has centred on the aristocracy and the upper-class élite groups, including financiers, traders, merchants, and businessmen in the south-east of England. It seems that these groups reaped the major rewards from the Empire in terms of profits from investments, posts in colonial administration, and senior positions in the army and navy. The members of both groups were the largest investors in the Empire and its major supporters in government, business and society.

The taxation system in Britain ensured that average middle-class taxpayers paid the major part of the cost of the defence and administration of the Empire. It was also the case that, unless such people worked in jobs related to the Empire or held profitable imperial investments, they gained nothing directly in return. However, large numbers of middle-class people signed up to fight in the Boer War, joined imperial societies and pressure groups, and were consumers of imperial literature. It is therefore clear that many people did not support the Empire because it was in their economic interest to do so.

The average working-class person was - as we have already seen - largely indifferent towards the Empire. But many of them benefited directly from its existence. In 1914 many working-class areas depended on the Empire for employment. The Lancashire cotton mills relied on the Indian market, and the shipbuilding yards in Portsmouth, Glasgow, Birkenhead, and Belfast were largely kept in work by the fact that a large navy was required for the defence of the Empire. But there were possible 'downsides'. By 1914 many people in the Liberal and Labour parties were arguing that the money being spent on the administration and defence of the Empire might be put to better use in alleviating the terrible problems of poverty, poor health, and sub-standard housing in Britain itself. It may also be worth adding that British industry may have been able to draw on a greater pool of investment had Britain abandoned the Empire prior to 1914. The problem here is deciding how much trade British industry would have retained had she given up the Empire. The example of the American colonies suggests a growth of trade. Yet in the years before 1914 it was probably more likely that if Britain had abandoned her empire many ex-colonies would have introduced protective tariffs against British goods or fallen under the control of other European powers who would also have introduced protectionism.

3 The Settlement Colonies

The British Empire served the interests of the colonies of settlement very effectively. They stand - even today - as the major beneficiaries from their links with Britain. Australia, Canada, New Zealand, and South Africa would not exist as viable states today without the vast amounts of investment they received from Great Britain between 1815 and 1914.

The granting of self-government allowed the settlement colonies to introduce tariffs to protect their own infant industries while, at the same time, they were still able to sell their goods in the free and open British market. Between 1860 and 1914 the colonies of settlement spent large sums of money on social reforms to benefit their residents, and they were allowed to raise loans to pay for this at advantageous rates of interest in the City of London. The British government offered guaranteed bonds to those who invested in the settlement colonies. It subsidised their administration charges and their shipping and telegraph cable links, and bore all the costs of their defence. They also received 66 per cent of all British investment within the Empire. This allowed their economies to develop rapidly. All the settlement colonies of the British Empire became very prosperous countries. In 1914 the Empire suited the interests of the settlement colonies very well.

4 The Dependent Empire

The story is somewhat different for the territories that made up the dependent empire. It is true that a case can be made for there being some definite gains for them in being colonised. For example, it is probable that the vast railway networks of India and much of Africa would not have been built had the British not been motivated to modernise the lands they controlled. And it is unlikely that the majority of the former British dependencies would have democratic constitutions and free elections today had they not become part of the Empire. In addition, British administrators established the rule of law and order in

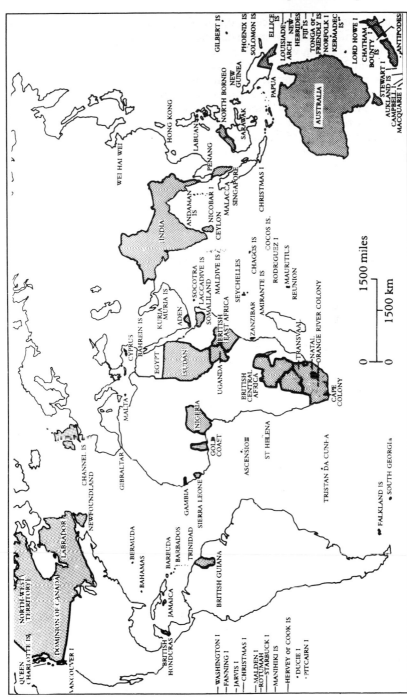

The British Empire in 1901

many areas where violence had previously been endemic. Even Gandhi, a bitter critic of British imperialism, did acknowledge that British rule modernised India, opened its people up to new ideas, and helped in the development of a 'New India'.

However, it is difficult to maintain that, on balance, being a part of the British Empire in 1914 was of benefit to the dependent territories. Although it cannot be quantified in financial terms, the 'non-white' inhabitants of the dependent empire had to suffer the indignity of being treated as inferiors during the whole of the period 1815 to 1914 and beyond. In economic terms, the situation was also unsatisfactory. For example, not only was India forced to pay 70 per cent of the cost of the British Indian army - essentially an army of occupation - but also the huge Indian market was forcibly kept open to British goods. As a result many of India's industries were destroyed and the country ran a huge trade deficit with Britain. All this has led many Indian historians to claim that if Britain had not run its Empire as a two-class system, and had treated India and the other dependencies in the same way as the settlement colonies, then the economic position of India and the other dependencies today would be completely different.

The argument that between 1815 and 1914 the British Empire primarily served the interests of white male élites, as many African, Indian and West Indian historians have claimed, is difficult to contradict. As Paul Gilroy puts it, the fact that 'there ain't no black in the Union Jack' illustrates a long-standing racial prejudice in the British attitude to the people of its Empire which has had a profound impact on race relations within Britain ever since. It is uncontestable that on the whole the people of the former dependent empire are still treated as not quite first-class citizens in modern British society. For this reason, if for no other, the history of the Empire remains very much an issue of the present as well as of the past.

Working on the 'Conclusion'

The main aim of this chapter has been to encourage you to think for yourself about who gained and who lost from the British Empire in the nineteenth century. What is important is that you form your own conclusions and that you are able to present evidence to support your views. The most useful task you could undertake after reading this chapter would be to make two lists - gainers and losers - and to explain in each case the way in which the group in question gained or lost. If you are taking a balanced view most groups should feature in both lists.

Chronological Table

1815   Congress of Vienna. France, Spain and Holland agreed to abolish the slave trade (Britain had done so in 1807).
Britain retained most of the colonial conquests made during the Napoleonic Wars, including the Cape of Good Hope (Holland received £6 million in compensation), Malta and Mauritius.

1834   Slavery abolished throughout the British Empire.

1837   Canadian Rebellion.

1838   May-December. Lord Durham's Mission to Canada.

1839   Durham Report recommended 'responsible government' for Canada.
'Opium War' between Britain and China began.

1840   Upper and Lower Canada united. New Zealand annexed.

1841   Robert Peel became British Prime Minister.

1842   Victory for Britain in 'Opium War'. China paid £13 million war indemnity, opened five ports, and ceded Hong Kong to Britain.

1843   Natal annexed.
Maori Wars against British rule in New Zealand began (British victory in 1847).

1846   Kaffraria and Labuan annexed. The Corn Laws repealed.

1848   Nova Scotia first colony with responsible ministry.
Responsible government implemented throughout Canada.
Transvaal and Orange Free State became Crown colonies.

1849   Navigation acts abolished.

1850   Australian Colonies Government Act.

1852   New Zealand Constitution Act.
Sugar duties abolished.

1855   New constitutions for most Australian colonies.

1857   May. Indian Mutiny began at Meerut - ended in 1858.

1858   British Columbia established.
November. Queen Victoria's Proclamation of British rule over India.
Government of India Act.

1859   Queensland became a separate colony.

1860   Second phase of Maori wars began - continued until 1870.

1861   Select Committee on Colonial Military Expenditure recommended cuts in British troops in colonies of settlement.
Lagos annexed.

1864   Britain ceded the Ionian Islands to Greece.

1865   Commons Select Committee on West African Settlements recommended 'no more annexations in West Africa'.

1867   British North American Act established 'Dominion of Canada'.
1868   Gladstone became Prime Minister for the first time.
1869   Suez Canal opened.
       The Hudson Bay Company ceded its right over territory to the
       government of the Dominion of Canada.
1871   British Columbia joined Dominion of Canada.
       Griqueland West (in South Africa) annexed following diamond
       discovery.
1872   Responsible government granted to Cape Colony.
       June. Disraeli delivered his famous Crystal Palace speech
       attacking Liberal 'indifference' towards Empire.
1873   Ashanti War began - ended in British victory.
1874   Disraeli became Prime Minister.
1875   Disraeli purchased Khedive of Egypt's stake in the Suez Canal
       Company.
1876   Queen Victoria created 'Empress of India'.
       Bulgarian atrocities.
1877   Transvaal annexed. Russo-Turkish War began.
1878   Congress of Berlin. Disraeli returned with 'Peace with Honour'.
       Afghan War began.
1879   Zulu War began - resulted in British victory.
       Gladstone embarked on his 'Midlothian Campaign' against
       Disraeli's 'imperialist mission'.
1880   March. Gladstone defeated Disraeli in general election.
       First Boer War began.
1881   Death of Disraeli (Lord Beaconsfield).
1882   British 'reluctant' occupation of Egypt.
1883   Lord Cromer appointed British agent and Consul-General in
       Egypt.
1884   November. Berlin West Africa Conference began. 15 nations
       attended. Decided ground rules for the Partition of Africa.
1885   Death of General Gordon at Khartoum.
       Indian National Congress founded.
1886   Gladstone defeated in general election over Irish Home Rule.
       Joseph Chamberlain and over 50 other Liberal MPs leave
       Liberal Party to join forces in a Unionist coalition with the
       Conservatives.
       Gold discovered in the Transvaal.
1888   Imperial British East Africa Company chartered.
1889   British South Africa Company chartered.
1890   British treaties with Germany and France concerning East and
       West Africa.
       Cecil Rhodes became Prime Minister of Cape Colony.

1893   Responsible government granted to Natal.
1895   Joseph Chamberlain appointed Colonial Secretary.
        The Jameson Raid ended in failure and 'humiliation' for Cecil
        Rhodes who resigned as Prime Minister of Cape Colony.
1896   Lord Kitchener advanced in the Sudan.
1897   Colonial Conference ended in failure.
        Lord Milner appointed High Commissioner for South Africa.
1898   Joseph Chamberlain announced five year economic plan to
        develop the West Indies.
        The Fashoda confrontation between Britain and France ended
        with France backing down. Britain now in full control of the
        Sudan .
        Lord Curzon became Viceroy of India.
        Death of Gladstone.
1899   October. Anglo-Boer War began.
        December. A 'black week' of British defeats in the Boer War.
1900   February. Lord Kitchener and Lord Roberts take command of
        British army in Boer War.
        Parrderg, Ladysmith, and Kimberly relieved by British forces.
        May. Relief of Mafeking sends British people wild with joy.
        Boxer Rebellion in China.
        October. Conservative victory in 'Khaki Election'.
1901   Worldwide outrage against British treatment of Boer prisoners of
        war.
        Queen Victoria died.
        Commonwealth of Australia formed.
1902   Boer War ended in British victory.
        Anglo-Japanese Alliance signed.
        Imperialism: A study by J.A. Hobson published.
1903   Joseph Chamberlain resigned as Colonial Secretary to form the
        Tariff Reform League.
1904   Anglo-French Entente signed.
1905   Bengal partitioned. Indian outrage.
        Lord Milner replaced as High Commissioner for South Africa.
1906   January. Liberal Party won landslide victory in general election.
1907   Anglo-Russia Convention signed.
        Responsible government granted to Orange River Colony.
1909   The Morley-Minto Reforms implemented in India.
        Indian Councils Act.
1910   Union of South Africa.
1914   August. First World War began.

Further Reading

The available literature on the British Empire from 1815 to 1914 is enormous. The following reading list is confined to a selection of books related to themes and regions discussed in individual chapters of the book. The more specialised texts are marked with an asterisk (*).

1 Introductory and General Texts

There are many worthwhile introductory and general texts. The most useful are: **P.J. Cain,** *The Economic Foundations of British Overseas Expansion 1880-1914,* (London 1980). **B. Porter,** *The Lions's Share: A Short History of British Imperialism 1850-1983,* (Longman 1987). **R. Hyman,** *Britain's Imperial Century 1815-1914,* (London 1975). A very good set of relevant essays is to be found in: **C.C. Eldridge,** ed., *British Imperialism in the Nineteenth Century,* (Macmillan 1984). Those wishing to pursue the topic in far greater depth should consult: * **P.J. Cain and A.G. Hopkins,** *British Imperialism: Innovation and Expansion 1688-1914,* (Longman 1993). This examines the role of 'gentlemanly capitalists' in British imperialism and is likely to become a 'classic' specialist text. * **D.K. Fieldhouse,** *Economics and Empire 1830-1914,* (London 1973). This is the best survey of the many theories and interpretations that have been advanced to explain the European empires in this period. * **M. Doyle,** *Empires,* (Cornell University Press 1987), is an excellent comparative analysis of empires. * **P. Kennedy,** *The Rise and Fall of the Great Powers: Economic Change and Military Conflict from 1500-2000,* (Fontana 1988), is a masterly account of the economics of great power conflict.

2 The Partition of Africa

There has been a veritable avalanche of books on every aspect of the Partition. The two most useful introductory texts for students are: **M.E. Chamberlain,** *The Scramble for Africa,* (Longman 1974), and **J.M. MacKenzie,** *The Partition of Africa,* (Routledge 1983).

3 Theories and Interpretations of Imperialism

The literature on the various theories and interpretations is enormous. The following are recommended for those studying the topic at undergraduate level. * **J.A. Hobson,** *Imperialism: A Study,* (London 1902). * **V.I. Lenin,** *Imperialism: The Highest Stage of Capitalism,* (1916). * **R. Owen and B. Sutcliffe** eds., *Studies in Theory of Imperialism,* (London 1972). * **R.E. Robinson and J. Gallagher** (with Alice Denny), *Africa and the Victorians: The Official Mind of Imperialism,*

(London 1961). This is probably the most influential study ever written on British imperialism. * **W.R. Louis,** ed., *Imperialism: The Gallagher and Robinson Controversy,* (London 1976), explores the controversy that the two great historians created. * **J.A. Schumpeter,** *The Sociology of Imperialism,* (London 1951). * **H.M. Wright,** *The New Imperialism,* (London 1961).

4 Individual Countries and Important Regions

The following are recommended to those studying the subject at undergraduate level who wish to enhance their knowledge of particular regions.

India: * **D. Kumar** ed., *The Cambridge Economic History of India Vol. II. 1760-1970,* (CUP 1983). China: * **M. Greenberg,** *British Trade and the Opening Up of China 1800-1842,* (CUP 1951). * **J. Fairbank** ed., *The Cambridge History of China, Vol X,* (Cambridge 1978), *Vol XI,* (Cambridge 1980). Canada: * **P. Burroughs,** *The Canadian Crisis and British Colonial Policy 1828-1841,* (London 1971). Australia: * **M. Dunn,** *Australia and the Empire: From 1788 to the Present Day,* (Sydney 1984). New Zealand: * **K. Sinclair,** *A History of New Zealand,* (London 1980). Africa: * **R.A. Oliver and G.N. Sanderson** eds., *The Cambridge History of Africa, 1870-1905, Vol VI,* (CUP 1985).

5 The Impact of Empire on British Politics and Society

a) Politics

For the role of Joseph Chamberlain see: **H. Brown,** *Joseph Chamberlain, Radical and Imperialist,* (Longman 1974). For Gladstone and Disraeli see **C.C. Eldridge,** *Imperialism in the age of Gladstone and Disraeli,* (London 1972). See also: **M. Winstanley,** *Gladstone,* (Routledge 1992) and **J. Walton,** *Disraeli,* (Routledge 1992). The most useful study of the Empire and British politics is: **R. Shannon,** *The Crisis of Imperialism,* (London 1977).

b) Popular Culture

In recent years there has been a large amount of very stimulating work on the impact of the Empire on popular culture. The most useful contributions have been:

* **J.M. MacKenzie,** *Propaganda and Empire: the Manipulation of British Public Opinion 1880-1960,* (Manchester University Press 1984), and * **J.M. MacKenzie,** ed., *Imperialism and Popular Culture,* (Manchester University Press 1986), which is a superb set of stimulating and readable essays.

6 The Boer War and its Consequences

The most comprehensive study of the Boer War is: **T. Pakenham,** *The Boer War,* (London 1979). For the impact of the war on Britain see: **R. Price,** *An Imperial War and The Working Class,* (London 1972).

7 The Costs and Benefits of Empire

The study of the costs and benefits of Empire has become a very important part of the debate. The whole question is examined in: * **L. Davies and R. Huttenback,** *Mammon and The Pursuit of Empire: The Political Economy of British Imperialism,* 1860-1912, (CUP 1986).

8 Document Collections

There are very few up-to-date and lively document collections on the Empire. The standard collection remains: **A.B. Keith** ed., *Speeches and Documents on British Colonial Policy 1763-1917,* (London 1966).

Index